A CAGE FOR ONE

A CAGE FOR ONE

Memoir of a Teenage Life

TINA FITZGERALD

© 2019 Tina Fitzgerald
All rights reserved. This book or any portion thereof may not be reproduced or used in any manner whatsoever without the express written permission of the publisher except for the use of brief quotations in a book review.
Published by Tina Fitzgerald
Book design and cover by Elite Authors
First Edition 2019
Printed in the United States of America
ISBN: 9781070653648

*To the ones who started this journey
and
to all the other little black birds learning to fly.*

Contents

Prologue: Time ix

Chapter 1	Secrets	1
Chapter 2	Caged	5
Chapter 3	Wraith	12
Chapter 4	Alone	17
Chapter 5	Believe	23
Chapter 6	Neglect	26
Chapter 7	Consequences	31
Chapter 8	Boys	37
Chapter 9	Darkness	43
Chapter 10	Light	46
Chapter 11	Hands	49
Chapter 12	Smitten	58
Chapter 13	Jackie	66
Chapter 14	Movies	70
Chapter 15	Desire	77
Chapter 16	Confession	82
Chapter 17	Misery	91
Chapter 18	Drugs	94

Chapter 19	Unicorns	97
Chapter 20	Mail	100
Chapter 21	Broken	102
Chapter 22	Wishes	109
Chapter 23	Refuge	115
Chapter 24	Reflection	118
Chapter 25	Requests	121
Chapter 26	Hello	125
Chapter 27	Pickles	130
Chapter 28	Numb	133
Chapter 29	Almost	137
Chapter 30	Toast	157
Chapter 31	Holidays	162
Chapter 32	Growing	169
Chapter 33	Separated	175
Chapter 34	College	178
Chapter 35	Empty	182
Chapter 36	Money	188
Chapter 37	Besties	191
Chapter 38	Stag	197
Chapter 39	Prom	203
Chapter 40	Home	210
Chapter 41	Graduation	214
Chapter 42	Freedom	220
Chapter 43	Peace	222
Acknowledgements		231

Prologue: Time

My memories of home are filled with people who had a way about them. A father's advice about love and life came from the Good Book. A mother fixed red beans and rice for dinner every Monday night. A grandmother called me "Petite Ba Bae," and a grandfather called me "Sha." A cousin taught me that snipe hunting was a practical joke and eating rattlesnake was the serious business of life or death.

I remember that life and progress was slow, and the pace of one's gait was equally so. I smile thinking about the way quiet would take over at sunset, and how the sidewalks would practically roll up at eight o'clock.

Home was Louisiana. The land of tooth-achy sweet tea, crawfish carcasses dancing on fingertips, and colorful Mardi Gras beads weighing down one's neck. Where respect is given by saying "ma'am" and "sir." Eye contact and a greeting are considered good manners among people passing on the street. Shortened words are twanged and drawled as strangers learn each other's life stories in grocery store checkout lines.

No, not New Orleans or a swamp full of alligators to hop over on the way to school. Central Louisiana. A twin city to be exact, but the Danny DeVito one, divided from the beefier sibling by a river the color of clay. Back when I was a kid, Interstate 49 didn't exist, and three bridges spanned the gap. Two of them stubbornly held onto their metal skeletons and looked like they would drop any moment in a foolhardy attempt to escape to the ocean.

Down the road from one of those bridges, I sat with ankles crossed on a concrete bench and stared at my high school parking lot. The outdoor senior area was the only place I could brood in solitude during lunch. No noise or frigid air-conditioning to contend with. The rows of cars rarely wavered from their spots as if anything to the contrary would result in all-out war. Bored with the perfected formation, I closed my eyes and turned my face to the heat of the sun. The year was 1996, and I looked forward to the end of my life.

I was the girl who rarely wore makeup and had a long tangle of hair that wasn't "Rachel" cut. The quiet and awkward one in Family Dollar Store clothes who smelled of cigarettes and had a master's degree in the art of resting bitch face. The one with a broken heart.

Unlike most teenagers, my time wasn't occupied with the trivial—fashion, parties, hanging out at the mall, and driving up and down Jackson Street for no damn reason. I cared for none of it—not that I had a choice. While my peers bemoaned the hardships of the average teenage life, I existed in an adult world with adult problems.

I lived day by day, not knowing what would happen next. Bad things were always one moment away, and I trusted no one. Only a carefully chosen few made it past my boundaries, and even then, access was a limited membership on a need-to-know basis.

Why?

Mother. The Breaker of Wills. The Flayer of Dignity. A cunning and charming siren whose blond hair, sharp blue eyes, and thin figure disguised her true nature—a beautiful disaster who fed on my love. I tried to be perfect. I did everything she wanted. Didn't matter. Her words still clawed and shredded and broke. The bruises and cuts always melted away to join the damage that no one could see.

Caged inside my own personal hell, I barely existed, yet I was no mere weak victim of circumstance. I knew there was more to life than the world Mother had created, so I kept both eyes on the future and where my actions could lead. High school became a means to an end, and graduation became my one obsession. A diploma was my golden ticket to freedom and a better life. With a white-knuckled grip, I desperately clung to hope, the only life preserver in the wake of Tsunami Mother.

That girl was my raw, authentic self. The one few people know about. The one I hated and spent two decades trying to hide within a barrier of shame. Ah, but I've gotten ahead of myself. I will start from the beginning. Time to shed light on those dark, chaotic years.

My secrets, my stories, the version of events that are mine and mine alone, are told as best as I can remember. To protect the identities of the people involved, many names and personal details have been altered or omitted.

CHAPTER 1

SECRETS

I always knew Mother was off. My suspicions gathered with pointed fingers until they shattered the last illusion. At six years old, I realized Mother had good days and bad days, and I worried as the bad ones multiplied like the horde of rabbits caged in our backyard. More and more, her daily routine consisted of her ear stuck to the house phone or random solo visits to the next-door neighbor's house. Meanwhile, my younger siblings and I ran around outside willy-nilly.

Arguments between my parents became the norm, especially when my father would come home from work at eight o'clock at night to find the house a mess and no one fed. He would start the laundry, make dinner, and then have words with Mother. When he came home early one day to find my two-year-old sister eating raw hamburger meat out of the refrigerator, the hushed spats behind closed doors became yelling and screaming all over the house. Shortly after, my parents doubled down and tried to work through their issues with violence. I alternated from trying to intervene in their battles to keeping Eric and Jenny occupied and out of the way, but no level of television volume could tune that out.

During the spring of 1986, I swore a vow of secrecy, and Mother shared her plan with me. "When Daddy goes to work, we are leaving and never coming back."

A few days later, Mother kept me home from school to help her prepare. I packed most of my clothes, but I had trouble deciding among my favorite toys. To the ones who had to stay behind, I whispered, "I'll be back for you soon." I tried to pack a bag full of books, but Mother said there wasn't enough room. She and her mysterious new friend, Richard, played *Tetris* with our belongings and stuffed our little car. Jenny was too small to understand what was happening. We checked Eric out of school and drove seven hours to my grandmother's house in Texas.

Less than a year later, Mother cajoled me into taking the witness stand during the nasty divorce. She said to me, "Tell them all the bad things Daddy did. Tell them, or you'll be taken away from me, and I'll never see you again."

Oh, the grip of fear and the failure to keep my sweaty hands from shaking as I spoke about the fights to a roomful of staring strangers. I shared our family secrets, which was forbidden ever since the night that seven-year-old me became afraid to tell.

⋏

Lined up on both sides of me, several stuffed animals stand guard atop my blue-and-white polka-dot blanket. They keep me safe from the terrible creatures I believe live in the dark. Shouts and an argument keep me somewhere between awake and dreams when my door opens.

Mother, angry but not yelling, says, "Tina Marie, why? Why did you do it?"

"What, Mommy?" I ask, confused, and rub my eyes as I look up at her. The light from the bathroom down the hall makes her somewhat visible.

"Did you tell anyone about what happens in our house?"

"What?" I reply, still not understanding, still half-asleep.

"You did something very bad, and now I have to spank you."

I see my father's leather belt in her hand and become afraid. I stay out of trouble as much as possible to avoid such punishments, especially from switches. Her previous statements race through my head. "But, Mommy, I only did what the commercial said! To tell someone if there's a problem! To get help if bad things happen!" I remain where I am, unsure of what to do.

"Who did you tell about me and Daddy?"

"I…I…I talked to Angela and her dad."

"What did you tell them?"

"That you and Daddy scream and yell at each other all the time and that he hits you."

"You shouldn't have told anyone!" she says, raising the belt, and I realize my father is in the doorway, watching us.

Mother hesitates, and he yells at her, "Do it!"

She strikes me twice across my legs, and I cry out more from surprise than pain, because the blanket protected me for the most part. I look up at her and scream that I'm sorry. She hesitates on the third strike, looks at my father, says she won't do it, and throws the belt on the floor before pushing past him.

He closes the door and follows her. They scream words I don't comprehend. I lie in shock, not understanding what happened, my brain going through the conversation I had last weekend with my best friend and her father. *How did they find out? It wasn't supposed to be like this. I was just trying to get help. I was so stupid to think anyone could help.*

My father barrels into my room and grabs the belt from the floor.

I scream, "Daddy!" as he throws back my covers, tossing my stuffed animals about the room, and hits me over and over. At first, I try to block the strikes, but my little hands and arms can't take it. I flail and twist around, my thin nightgown useless, the snapping sound a chorus with my screams.

I don't know how many times he hit me or when he stopped. Consumed by the fire on my skin, I eventually realize that he's gone, that only my head is untouched, and that at some point I curled up into a ball. I do know the words he yelled at me with each hit, words I repeat in my head over and over until sleep finally takes me.

"Don't ever tell anyone! Never tell! This is our family! What happens in this house is no one's business! Don't you ever tell anyone ever again!"

CHAPTER 2

CAGED

Father disappeared to Chicago and never looked back. Mother got full custody and went through a string of boyfriends. My siblings and I spent a few years bouncing back and forth between wherever she lived and my grandmother's house. The racquetball game ended when Mother met Kevin, and the five of us moved back to our old neighborhood in Louisiana. For a few years, we lived in relative harmony, until Jim and his mustache entered the picture, and Kevin got kicked to the curb.

Life became harder for me when Mother and Jim suddenly combined households. We moved out to the middle of nowhere, and I was forced to switch junior high schools halfway through seventh grade. Plus, my responsibilities multiplied by two; I suddenly had another brother and sister who were the same ages as Eric and Jenny.

During that time, I hit puberty, and Mother simultaneously completed her transformation to batshit crazy.

With the most cheerful demeanor possible, I instantly respond to all of Mother's requests and demands. Cook, clean, do extra chores, wait on her hand and foot. All the ass-kissing and careful negotiations earn me a week with Stella during Thanksgiving break.

My cousin Stella has been a best friend of mine for as long as I can remember. Our mutual love of mermaids and unicorns sealed our friendship when we were little. A year older than me, she's the big sister I always wanted, and I admire her immensely. She's beautiful, smart, and popular. Other than our fair skin, we are complete opposites. She's taller, with blond hair and green eyes—more like Mother than I could ever be. I inherited the dark hair and eyes of my Filipino father.

During my vacation with Stella, I am my true self—just another silly thirteen-year-old girl having fun. She lets me dress up in her clothes. We put on makeup and crimp each other's hair. Our hysterical laughter from late-night Uno and gin rummy battles often wakes her parents. In the living room, we dance and sing along to nonstop MTV music videos. We play Nintendo, talk about boys, and get moon-eyed over Keanu Reeves.

On Tuesday, the phone rings, and Uncle Henry answers. He hands me the phone. No amount of pleading from me or reasoning from him will change my fate. Mother cuts my week of freedom short by two days.

While my Aunt Susan drives me home, I feel extra prickly at the thought of returning to my cage. *Should have known it wasn't gonna last. Guess she got tired of doing everything herself, or she decided it was a bad idea to leave four children unsupervised. This is bullshit!*

The closer we get, the angrier I become, but my rebellious thoughts are often interrupted. I must guide my aunt through the maze of Camp Livingston, a wooded area that used to be an old military base.

When the car stops in front of the house, I see Mother and Jim lounging in chairs on the front porch. Stella gets out of the car because I'm wearing her Hypercolor clothes, and I need to change. Her Royal Highness eyeballs me as we walk up the sidewalk. *Oh, here we go.*

I stop in front of the patio table, and Stella stops behind me at the top of the porch steps. Jim gives me a warning face. Mother doesn't even say hello. Stella nervously says to me, "I can just get them from you later."

Before I can respond, Mother drills me with questions. I say to her, "What do you mean, where have I been? I've been at Uncle Henry's house." I give her a summary of events, but then she demands to know why I've been gone so long. "Mom, you said I could be gone for a week, which isn't for two more days," I remind her.

"I never said you could be gone for a week," she corrects me.

"Okay? You're the one that called me yesterday and told me I had to come home early, remember?"

"So, fat ass, you're going to be disrespectful on top of it? Don't correct me."

"Mom, why do you have to be so mean? I'm not trying to be disrespectful. I'm just…never mind." I sigh and ask, "What do you need me to do?"

She rattles off a short list and orders me to get my fat ass moving.

You got to be kidding me. "So, you made me come home early to do the laundry and clean the house. Can't you ever do anything yourself?" I say, unable to stop the words from jumping out of my mouth.

"You fucking little cunt," Mother says and as quick as an asp, she launches over the patio table and slaps me right in the face. "You think just because Stella is here, you can say whatever you want to me! Well, say goodbye to her, 'cause you're never going over there again!"

I turn to Stella, who stares at my mother like a deer in headlights. "Go," I say to her, but I don't see her leave, because Mother grabs my arm and drags me into the house. The entire time, she graciously belittles me with every version of "ugly, fat whore" she can scream. After she slams the door, I wrestle my arm out of her grip and scream right back, "Leave me the fuck alone!"

"How dare you!" she shrieks and smacks the hell out of my face.

I'm not taking this shit anymore! I strike back and have five full seconds of joy and satisfaction as I watch the look of shock on her face and see my red handprint appear like a neon sign.

The real brawling begins. She slaps and kicks, but she's slower and skinnier than me, and my fists are up for the challenge. *To hell with the slapping!* There's a song of fury in my heart, and I gleefully kick my mother's ass.

Devious and without honor, she grabs for my hair, but I dodge and kick her shin. She goes for my hair again, but this time I can't move fast enough. *That's so cheating!* With control of my head, she punches me in the eye. I stomp on her foot in return, and she loses her grip.

I forcefully shove her away from me. She flies backward and struggles to stay upright. I tackle her to the floor and straddle her waist. Trapped beneath me, she digs her long nails into my forearms and tries to bite me like a goddamned cat while I attempt to control her arms. She twists and thrashes, which almost throws me off, but her efforts scoot me forward. I pin her arms under my legs and slap her in the face. I cackle. "How does it feel, you crazy bitch?"

I'm all slappy hands, and the revenge is sweet. She curses me and spews forth every dark and foul word her decrepit soul can form. Her eyes bulge above her strawberry cheeks. I want to shove my thumbs into her eye sockets so I will never be forced to look into those blue demon orbs again.

Instead, I grab her throat with both hands. *The world needs peace and quiet from this beast.* She thrashes more, legs kicking, but I squeeze harder and enjoy the ride. I tell her, "Die, bitch."

I'm seriously going to enjoy murdering her, and when she is finally still and quiet, I'll gouge her eyes out and stomp on them. Then I'll have a party with the rest of the world to celebrate that the wicked witch is dead.

"Tina. Stop. Please," she manages to say in a garbled whisper. Her face comes into focus. Tears run into her ears. My hands freeze.

This is my mother. I love her. Love and honor thy mother. I don't want to kill her. I want her cruelty and malice to stop. She's my mother. I don't want the police and lawyers. I don't want to ruin my life over this psycho.

Tears trickle down my face, and my thumbs relax.

I've never had a violent bone in my body. I've gone crazy. This isn't me. This is her. I've become her. She's turned me into her. Shame. What have I done? White-hot shame. There's a vicious, murderous creature wearing my skin.

Sobs erupt, and my hands try to hide the burning shame. I completely release her from my control and remain crouched on the floor. When her legs disappear from beside me, I stare at the blurry floor through watery eyes. She squats a few feet ahead of me. The sounds of her broken breaths make me cringe. "I'm sorry," I say and look up to see rage and madness on her face.

She rushes and tackles me. The back of my head hits the floor, and for a moment, I see stars. Our roles now reversed, she strikes both sides of my face. My head whips from side to side as her open hands fly left and right.

Keep fighting! Don't let her win! Kill this sorry excuse for a human being! Wipe her from the earth!

My body continues to writhe and scream, refusing to accept defeat, but... *No. I give up. I won't be like her. I won't become her. I won't turn into some rage-filled monster that finds joy and triumph in dominance and violence.*

My lip bursts, which I only know because my mouth fills with a coppery, metallic taste. I eventually gain control over my rebellious body and become still. She continues to hit me because my noncompliant mouth curses and screams.

"Tina, stop!" she orders, but my mouth refuses to concede, so she repeatedly hits me on the right side of my face and tells me to stop after each shriek of "I hate you!"

From somewhere in the room, Jim says to her, "Stop. She's done. You've won."

I become silent and wait for what Mother will do next. She lowers her hand and says, "I'll let you up if you stop."

I can barely breathe from her weight on my chest. I'm tired.

"Are you going to stop?" she asks.

I rasp out a feeble yes. Air returns to my lungs, and I get out a last "I hate you."

CHAPTER 3

WRAITH

The numbness in my mind leaves me disconnected from my body as I lay prone and still on the floor for a long time. Eventually, I notice the comforting darkness behind my closed eyes. I turn my face to the side and feel a strange heaviness on both sides of my head. My fingers locate the pooled tears in my hair, and I begin to assess the damage by the amount of pain I feel.

I open my eyes and sit up. The room spins a few times, but at least I no longer have blood on my tongue. Mother's not in the living room or the kitchen. I'm alone.

I crouch and stand. My limbs are heavy, as if I'd jumped in a swimming pool fully clothed and climbed up a side ladder. With achy hands, I straighten and dust off Stella's T-shirt and shorts. My forearms are peppered with red, crescent moon–shaped indentions and long, thin scratches. There are small, random bruises on my hands, arms, and legs, except for the large one forming on my calf where Mother kicked me.

I limp to the bathroom and lock the door behind me. As I turn on the faucet, I look in the mirror and see a wraith staring back at me with wide, red-rimmed eyes. Warm, salty tears leak into my gaping mouth. *Crying isn't going to make it any better.*

A few splashes of cold water later, I pat my face with a clean towel, careful to avoid the gash that is my bottom lip. *Better work on the blood first.* I hold a washrag under the running water and then place it against my mouth. My eyes protest with watery shouts. Images of *Tom and Jerry* cartoons pop into my head, and I no longer find humor in Tom's smashed fingers, toes, and tail.

After I scrub the smeared, dried blood from my chin, I move my lips around. Their range of motion is enough to rinse out my mouth. I cautiously tongue the inside of my cheeks and find grooves and ridges that mirror my teeth. A swallow of water and a round of gargling helps soothe what's left of my throat.

My cheeks and jaw appreciate the cool, somewhat bloody washrag that flitters about. Red traces disappear down the drain with each rinse. Bruises bloom across my face and decorate my left eye. With brush in hand, I ignore the anger from my tender scalp and straighten my disheveled hair. Gobs of me decorate the floor.

I debate taking a shower. All I really want to do is sleep, so I wash my arms and look in the medicine cabinet. My choices are rubbing alcohol and Merthiolate antiseptic. I curse and blow on my cuts as I cover them with orange liquid fire.

When I'm done, I ninja from the bathroom to my bedroom without seeing anyone. I change clothes and toss Stella's torn and orange-smudged shirt in the garbage. Under the relative safety of my sheet and blanket, I barely finish my last thought before passing out. *I hate that my door locks from the outside.*

⋏

I cautiously enter the kitchen the next morning. Jim says to me, "You look better than she does," and gives me a pat on the top of my head. "You had her. Why did you give up?"

"I didn't want to turn into her," I tell him.

He looks at me with sympathy, hands me a steak from the fridge for my eye, and says, "I'll cook that for you when you're done."

Mother's holed up in her room. I watch, One-Eyed Willy style, from the end of the hallway as the rest of the kids wait on her hand and foot. *Good. I'm off duty.*

When they finish serving her, they enter the kitchen to begin their own breakfasts. One after the other, they momentarily stop in the doorway when they realize what they missed yesterday. I take a seat at the table and concentrate on the sizzling sound of my steak in a skillet. I ignore the stolen glances in my direction as boxes of cereal of are opened and milk is poured. Jim's son, who gives Mother hell at any opportunity, sits right next to me and breaks the silence when he asks, "Was it worth it?"

A ghost of a smile has him grinning.

⋏

Peace and quiet permeate the house until Sunday afternoon. Mother finally emerges, moving like a gimpy turtle into the kitchen. I watch her until she looks at me. *Sheesh. Jim was right.*

I stare at the wall and await my punishment. For a week, I must clean the whole house every day by myself; otherwise, I'm to stay in my room with meals brought to me, and no phone calls. For good measure, she tacks on that I can't go anywhere on the weekends for a month, and Stella's house is forbidden.

Nothing new. Jim must have had something to do with why I'm not being flayed alive. Joke's on her. She forgets that every time I'm imprisoned in my room, it's a vacation for me. The rest of the kids will do her bidding without me.

⋏

As I wait for the school bus beside our open front door, Mother says to me, "You're not going to wear any makeup?"

The bus pulls up, and I say, "Nope. I'm going as is, so the world can see what you did." I walk out the door, and she doesn't follow.

On the bus, I am immediately questioned. Filled with shame at the cause of my injuries, I choose to lie to all my friends with a cockamamy story about getting into a go-carting accident on the wooded dirt trails around my house.

"No, I wasn't strapped in. No, I wasn't wearing a helmet. Yes, the cart flipped over. Yes, the scratch marks are from when I landed in the bushes," I reply to a barrage of questions from everyone except my teachers, who don't say a word. They all believe me except the bus driver, who doesn't let me off the bus until I swear on my mother's life that the flimsy story is true.

⋏

Imprisonment ends right on schedule. My wounds are healed, and I am free to flee on the weekends, but my act of mercy comes at a price. Mother has me caged. I resolve to be timid, quiet, and obedient. Never question. Never rebel. Her authority is absolute, and her wrath is more than I can bear.

My mind won't let go, and I relive the fight over and over. The compulsive thoughts and feelings drive me mad. I'm hypervigilant and jumpy around people. Unable to focus, I find myself standing still in the middle of mundane tasks. Sleep is difficult to find.

No more playing chase in the rain or spinning wildly on the tire swing. There's no joy when I gather eggs from the chicken coop. I pick corn and snap beans for dinner and no longer feel pride in the garden I helped Jim plant.

Doubt creeps in. *I deserve to be punished for my wickedness.* Self-hatred gnaws at my insides. I become the wraith in the mirror.

CHAPTER 4

ALONE

Four months after I'm caged, Mother's relationship with Jim burns like a grease fire, and we are back in "where to live" limbo. Until Mother can move us back to our old neighborhood, she arranges for me to finish eighth grade at my original junior high school. On Wednesdays and Fridays, I am to walk to Tom's house after school and wait there until she gets off work.

Mother has known Tom for over twenty years. My siblings and I have known him for the last four years, and we consider him an uncle. From time to time, Mother and I visit where he works, and she usually makes me walk around the store, away from the front counter. I find her instructions extremely suspicious. On one such occasion, I caught her stuffing a bag of pot into her purse.

On the first day, Tom shows me around the house and tells me to make myself at home. I'm allowed to do whatever I want except touch the weapons, let the snake out, or make long-distance phone calls. If there's an emergency, he's only a few blocks down the street.

Mother's timely arrivals proceed directly to often late. On the days Mother neglects to show at all, Tom drives me to Camp Livingston, and we find her there. If not, I have no clue where she is or what she's doing. I don't bother to ask anymore. She has never been consistent with anything. Perhaps she has been that way her entire life.

With three hours to spare and the house to myself, I finish my homework and spend the remainder of the afternoon trying to escape boredom. I rarely have free time, much less alone time, and I don't know what to do with myself. Friends are rarely home to answer their phones. If I'm lucky, I'll find a television show to watch, but pickings are slim with only four clear channels. Next, I battle the old radio record player. At sloth speed, I turn the dial back and forth in search of hidden music on the number line. Most of the time, I get either static or country music; defeated, I flip the knob to off.

If I'm really bored, I peruse his strange hodgepodge of books lining several shelves. I open three out of curiosity but put them back because I feel like a snoop, and some are inappropriate. I look at his collection of firearms displayed on the walls and wonder if they've ever been used. When the snake isn't dreaming about what I assume to be rabbits and freedom, I watch its giant, dark form slither about the equally gigantic glass tank. I'm free to eat anything in the fridge, but apparently bachelors only eat ketchup and bologna sandwiches. As a last resort, I open the fridge door, just in case there is a change of scenery inside.

After four mindless days, looping through each activity, I admit to Tom that I'm bored. The next Wednesday, he offers to pay me to clean the house, water his assortment of dogs, and push mow the lawn. I've heard stories about kids earning money for chores and can't believe I'm one of them. He hands me a twenty-dollar bill, and I examine the green paper like it's a rock from the moon. I put the treasure in my back pocket and plan to hide its existence from Mother.

I learn to embrace quiet solitude and the simple events that I once found mindless. I enjoy over a month of peaceful afternoons without Her Majesty yelling and degrading and demanding and expecting. My earnings are stashed in several places around my room to thwart her pirating efforts.

On the days I'm covered in grime, grass bits, and sweat, I enjoy a bath in the large, white clawfoot tub. A blade or two of grass always swirls around me. Tendrils of steam rise up from the water. Eyes closed, I rest my head and listen to the hum of the cicadas. When prune fingers and toes wiggle at me, I reluctantly leave my watery haven.

On a Friday, during one such blissful bath, Tom opens the bathroom door behind me and strolls right in. Even though my back is to him, I curl up and cover what I can of my front. He doesn't immediately apologize or leave, so I say, "Hello! I'm taking a bath here!" Over my shoulder, I see him standing motionless by the sink, less than ten feet away from me. I glance at my too-far-away towel perched on a stool beside the tub. "Uh, get out!" I yell.

Without a word, he walks out. I quickly dry off and put on my clothes. When I crack the door open, I see him waiting on the couch. I enter the living room, and he begins a barrage of apologies. He didn't realize I mowed the grass today, and he's just used to going anywhere in the house, and he will make sure to knock if the door is closed, and on and on. I tell him okay and that no harm was done.

⊥

Two weeks later, I attempt to lock the bathroom door. The off-kilter knob won't stay latched and prevents the door from closing completely. I look at the curtainless tub sitting in the middle of the bathroom and debate what to do. Tom's workday is far from over, the tub is full of water, and I'm already partially undressed. I decide to make it quick.

With a lather of bubbles running down my forehead, I take a breath to go under the water; I freeze. Tom's footsteps make their way to the bathroom door. Two short knocks and an "I'm coming in to talk to you" precede him. I curl into a ball.

In one quick movement, he moves the stool and towel from their location next to the tub and makes himself comfortable two feet from the faucet in front of me. His lips move. Something about the dogs and the lawn mower. I concentrate on the towel in his hands, and words that I don't remember come out of my mouth.

"Okay. That's all I wanted to know. I'll see you when you get out." He stands, puts the stool and my towel back in place, and leaves.

Unsure what to do or say or think, I sit, unmoving, until a shiver passes through me. I rinse my hair in the cold water and pull the drain plug. The gurgling noise keeps time as I barely dry off and throw on my clothes.

I stick my head out the door and find that I'm alone. He'd said something about coming home for a second to get something someone wanted to buy, which makes no sense until I realize it may have been pot. I pray to God for my mother to pick me up, but of course, she's a no-show.

⊥

Tom drives me to the new house, which we should be fully moved into next week. I usually wear the house key on a silver chain around my neck, but it is now wrapped several times around my wrist. During the ten-minute drive, I sit as far away from him as the pickup truck cabin will allow. I'm silent while he tries to make small talk like nothing happened. *Does he think I'm my mother, and this kind of shit is appropriate?*

Naturally, no one is home. When we stop in the driveway, I pull the door latch, but instead of the metal door squealing open, I hear the *kerchunk* of the locks trapping me.

"Tom, what are you doing?"

"I thought we could talk before you go in," he says and scoots closer to me.

"You talked the whole way here. I have nothing to say to you." I squeeze closer to the door and unlock it, but he locks it again. "Tom, let me out," I demand.

"You've grown up to be very beautiful," he states.

"Yep. Now let me out!"

He tries to kiss me.

"Stop!" I shout and dodge.

He leans away from me and says, "Don't tell your mother about anything that happened. It's not nice to tease older men."

The accusation immobilizes me. He grabs the front of my shirt.

"No!" I yell and push his hand away from me. My hands find their marks, and I jump out of the truck. The door slams in his face, and I run to the house. I concentrate on the key and the deadbolt, and my hands obey despite their trembling. I immediately shut and lock the front door behind me. My heart tries to burst out of my chest.

We have no phone. Aunt Evelyn, Mother's best friend, lives five blocks away, but I don't want to leave the safety of the house. I sit with my back against the door even after he drives off.

What if he followed me in here? Did I do this? Is this my fault? Did I tease him like he said? I must have done something wrong. This is my fault. What was I thinking? I should have never been in that bathtub. I was alone in a grown man's house. That's Mother's friend. I can't tell her. What if he tells her what I did? What kind of punishment will I get? Thank God I don't have to see him for another five days. I have time to figure out what to do.

I stay where I am until Mother comes home forty-five minutes later in a foul mood. I try to tell her what happened, but she's busy with yelling and smacking me because my chores aren't done.

CHAPTER 5

BELIEVE

On Sunday morning, Mother says to me, "I have to finish moving our stuff. I can't pick you up from school tomorrow."

I panic.

"Mom, I don't want to go to his house anymore. I'm bored, and all I do is sit around for three hours."

She tells me that this is the last week.

"Mom, please, I can't go over there anymore."

She doesn't listen and waves me away with an annoyed grunt. I follow her around the living room and ask, "Can I go home with Stella for the week?"

She yells that I'm trying to weasel my way back to Stella's house even though I'm forbidden to do so since our fight. Risking further wrath, I calmly state, "I refuse to go, and I'll stay at school until someone comes to get me."

Her aim is not quite right, and she pops me in the ear instead of the face. Over the pain and ringing, I scream, "I'm not going!"

She grabs my hair and slings me into my room. The door slams shut and locks. I hold my ear and sob into the floor that I won't go.

An hour later, I bang on the door and yell that I need to go to the bathroom. She unlocks the door and stands in the doorway with a controlled, calm face. In a pleasant voice, she says, "Why don't you want to go to Tom's? I thought you liked going over there."

Avoiding her eyes, I say to her, "I was taking a bath, and he… he walked in. The first time, he said it was an accident, but the second time, he did it on purpose. He sat there talking to me, and I didn't know what to do."

She says nothing and stares at me with a gaping mouth.

I beg, "Mom, please. Please don't make me go over there. Please. I'm scared of him."

The usual glare forms on her face. "You lie," she accuses. The door shuts and locks.

I sit on my bed in disbelief and cover my mouth with a hand. *She doesn't believe me. She doesn't believe me? She doesn't believe me!* I bang on the door, rattle the knob, and yell repeatedly, "Mom, I swear, I'm telling the truth! Why would I lie? I have no reason to lie! Why won't you believe me? I'm telling the truth!"

The door abruptly opens and halts against my shoulder. She grabs her favorite handle and guides me to the middle of the living room. We kneel as she pulls one side of my face to the floor. I plead with her the whole time over her screams of "You lying little bitch! You lie!"

I do my best to look her in the eyes. "Why would I lie? Why would I lie? Why would I go to all this trouble not to go there?"

She releases my hair. I sit up and explain between sobs, "That's not all of it. When he dropped me off on Friday, he tried to kiss me, and then he tried to put his hand up my shirt. He told me not to tell you. He told me that I teased him."

Scooting backward and away from me, she says, "You lie. I've known him for most of my life. He would never do such a thing."

"Mom, I swear, I didn't do anything wrong! Why would I lie? Why would I make all this up? I've never lied to you before. Why would I do this now?" *It doesn't ever matter; lies or the truth, I'm still punished. Always punished, no matter what.* I say to her, "You're my mother. You're supposed to believe me."

She continues to sit on the floor in silence.

"She's supposed to believe me," I say out loud as I stand and finally go to the bathroom.

On the way back to my room, I pass through the living room and see Mother on the couch. In the doorway, she comes up behind me, and I brace myself for another assault. She hugs me from behind and says, "I believe you."

I go home with Stella for the rest of the week.

CHAPTER 6

NEGLECT

Summer and my fourteenth birthday come and go, and thus begins my freshman year of high school. My best friend, Iris, and I, along with Chloe and Amber, continue to be friends from junior high and form a close-knit group. We join the color guard and are constantly together. Life becomes a blur of Friday night football games, sleepovers at Iris's house, figuring out boys and algebra, and the homecoming dance.

↟

Mother does her best to be a model parent, and we enjoy a life of relative stability and structure. She often cooks dinner, cleans the house, and spends time with us kids. Several nights a week, she kisses my forehead and wishes me good night.

Sans shoes, my siblings and I spend our free time outside with a dozen other kids of various ages. Bikes are ridden from one end of the neighborhood to the other, with races down the road with the steep hill. We injure each other during sweet gum ball wars and take turns drinking straight from the water hose.

We capture little green lizards that scurry across the porch and window sills. Eric hangs them from his earlobes. I play with daddy longlegs and laugh at the wide-eyed little kids who watch the harmless creatures crawl up and down my arms. In the empty lot across the street, fierce kickball games end with a scramble of arms and legs to the top of the giant sycamore tree. Once the sun goes down, we play hide-and-seek across three front yards.

My favorite place is behind our neighborhood, just a hop over our backyard fence—the forest. Alone, I sometimes wander the natural trails just to see what I can find. Every shade of green surrounds me. Bright, golden light filters between branches to illuminate patches of the forest floor. I notice flowers and mushrooms and intricate lacy webs. I stand still and listen to the call of birds and the wind dancing through the treetops.

Most of the time, a troupe of us make a racket on the way to the wide, muddy creek. We cross over fallen logs or walk through shallow, pebbly places where driftwood stands like dark sailboats anchored in the water. We keep our eyes peeled for the specific landmarks that lead to our swimming hole. Go left and down the hill. Pick up the trail, and take the right fork. Pass the giant oak, and turn left into the chest-high, feathery bushes.

As with all things Mother, our happy life slowly changes back to chaos. I soon give up on any expectations and morph back into the role of parent. When she becomes unofficially involved with Jim, everyone immediately upgrades to the express crazy train. Her late arrivals home progress to complete absences for up to three or four days at a time. We never know when she'll be gone, and she refuses to discuss where she's been. I eventually sleep in my own bed after several nights of pointlessly falling asleep in her bed with hope that she'll come back.

I wake Eric and Jenny, make sure they are presentable, and watch as they get on the school bus. A few minutes later, I get on mine, thankful to escape to a better place. In the afternoons, we arrive home about the same time. If my bus is late, they wait for me by the front door unless Mother is home. I clean the house and figure out dinner. After I help Eric and Jenny with their homework, they take showers and go to bed on time. I do my homework, double-check the door locks, and turn out the lights.

Food becomes scarce. I ration and hope the portions are good for one more day. I eat the oldest food and learn what to avoid by trial and error. Hunger has an order that I learn to expect. Cereal until there's no milk, then dry cereal until the boxes are empty. Canned creamed corn or green beans until the shelf is bare. Slices of plastic-covered American cheese until the empty wrapper that used to hold the stack stares right back at us. Ketchup sandwiches until there's no bread, which means ketchup and crackers, until finally, we eat spoonfuls of ketchup. There's nothing like standing in front of an open, empty refrigerator and trying to decide what to feed myself and two other children.

We wait fifteen more minutes before beginning our meager dinners, just in case Mother randomly appears with groceries. When she does show up, we complain about her leaving us alone, especially without food. If she has groceries, she makes a joke and says that everything is fine now. If she comes home empty-handed, she begs our forgiveness and promises to be better. When she comes home after the third time we go to bed with empty bellies, Eric threatens to call the cops. We tell her that we would rather live with Father. Her response?

"I've sacrificed everything for us to keep our family together, and y'all are cruel to want to leave me," she sobs. "Go ahead, call the police! See what happens to you out there in the world, where I can't protect you! You don't know how scary and dangerous the world is. We have to stick together to stay safe."

She claims foster care is worse. The three of us will end up separated out in the world with strangers, and we will never see each other again. She repeats her other usual warning. "Your only alternative is to move far away to a strange city and your horribly abusive father."

After that day of hysterics, Mother gets a bright idea. No, she doesn't leave us fully stocked with groceries. When two family-sized Little Caesars pizzas get dropped on the kitchen counter, we know she will vanish the next day. Pizza for breakfast. Pizza for lunch. Pizza for dinner. I give up trying to warm it in the oven and eat it cold, right out of the box.

I remain compliant and play Mother's game of neglect with a side of pizza. Every evening, my brave face washes down the bathroom sink. The wraith in the mirror watches as I brush my hair and teeth. I turn off my bedroom light and crawl deeper inside myself. I lie in bed and try to silence the chaos in my head. *What did I do to deserve this life? I do everything right, and still I suffer. Why can't she just love us? Why can't we be enough?*

I awake each morning with hope of a better day. For my siblings, I put on a smile and a sunny disposition like an old coat. Eventually, I free-fall into the rabbit hole of despair. When I reach the bottom, I discover a humble friend. She cushions my crash landing and stands me upright. Anger. Just a smidge. Just an ember. But I find it and hold on.

The earliest of memories flood my mind like a torrential downpour during a Louisiana sunshiny day. *My godfather, Byron. Kindness, affection, and laughter. My feet on his as we danced in the living room. Hot chocolate and campfires. The boat on the lake. Him teaching me how to clean our catch. Church and holding hands as we crossed the street. The joy on his face when I saw snow for the first time. The feel of his arms as he carried me home after trick-or-treating the whole neighborhood. Watching from the windows as he traveled around the house on the riding lawnmower. The smell of grease while he worked on his truck engine. Never doubting that I am loved.*

My anger blazes into determination. I make promises. *I won't be her. I won't let her win. I will be better than her. I will have a better life.*

CHAPTER 7
CONSEQUENCES

After lunch on a Thursday in February, Amber and I go to class, and I sit at my desk for all of five minutes before I'm called to the front office. As I make my way down to the first floor, I wonder if I'm somehow involved in trouble someone else got into or if I will get an award, because report cards are coming out soon.

No such luck.

The counselor and the assistant principal tell me that there was an incident with Mother and that I'm moving to Dallas to live with my grandmother. Despite my hysteria, they refuse to explain exactly what happened.

I shuffle to my locker. In the deserted hallway, I gather my belongings and stare at the empty metal space. I think about how I won't know Scott beyond the three days he escorted me to and from several classes—he was the whole reason I figured out the rules of football. My ever-so-clever best friend, Iris, had to be the reason he suddenly popped up at my locker and talked to me.

⋏

Dressed in our color guard uniforms, my best friends and I sit in the stadium bleachers during a home game. When the marching band is silent, and our flags lie motionless, Iris, Chloe, and Amber talk. With glances and nods, I half pay attention to their conversations. I move up one row for a better view and to escape scrutiny every time I cheer.

Iris plops down right next to me. Amber and Chloe scooch over and lean in behind us. I keep my eyes on the field and hope they'll give up easily, like the last time Iris got suspicious.

"Okay, so who is it?" Iris asks.

"Who's what?" I ask innocently.

"Who do you like?"

"What makes you think I like someone?" I turn to her with my full attention.

"Tina, no one actually watches the games unless they like someone."

I'm busted, so I give her a grin and say, "Number seventeen."

Chloe asks, "Who's number seventeen?"

They all look in Amber's program. "Scott!" they exclaim.

"Yep," I confirm, with a big smile.

"When did this start?" Chloe asks.

"Well, she has been paying attention for a couple of months," Amber answers.

I explain, "Yeah. I saw him that day we waited for the football team to finish so the band could practice on the field." I replay in my mind how he ran right past me. I couldn't keep my eyes off of him. His teammate noticed and pointed me out. Scott looked for me in the crowd, but I maneuvered around people and kept out of sight. The next day, back on the sidelines of the field,

I stood where he could easily find me. He smiled back until his teammate elbowed him because he wasn't following the line of players into the building.

With my attention back on the row of uniforms and my eyes in pursuit of that special number, I hear Chloe ask, "Isn't he the hot one?" to which Iris replies, "Yes. Tall, blond, blue eyes. She has a type."

"I do not!" I deny with a giggle, and everyone jumps up with a cheer as the receiver catches a perfect throw and runs for the end zone.

⋏

I follow the directions from the assistant principal and return the textbooks to my teachers, most of whom are surprised and sympathetic. After our science teacher allows us a moment in the hallway, I quickly tell a confused Amber that I'm moving to Dallas and ask her to tell the others. She has a thousand questions that mirror my own, but we simply hug goodbye. I continue like a snail back to the office in an attempt to delay the inevitable.

A worried and confused Stella finds me in the hallway and explains that she was called down to the office to say goodbye. She says that she waited for me and volunteered to find me because I was taking too long. I give her what little information I have. Her face fills with pity, and she hugs me tightly.

⋏

My siblings and I end up at Aunt Evelyn's house until our grandmother can pick us up. Eric and I see Mother on the evening news, and we piece together what happened.

Mother's disappearing acts finally caught up with her. Since we often lacked food, our two dogs in the backyard sure as hell didn't have any either. When the dog food ran out, we shared what we had with them, and when there wasn't enough, they lived on water. Not surprisingly, one of them died while we were at school, and the neighbors called the cops. Mother was promptly arrested. The police found her at a gas station, filling up her car.

⊥

After packing what I can fit of my belongings into a few small boxes, I beg my grandmother for a chance to say goodbye to all my friends. For one hour on Saturday evening, she waits in the parking lot of Clubb's Skating Rink.

During the winding drive through every Podunk town, I sit in the back seat and stare at the passing dark landscape. I swear I'll never show interest in another guy, because life is too shameful with Mother and too chaotic with all the moving. As we pass through the city of Natchitoches, I fall asleep with my wet face against the window frame.

⊥

For like the hundredth time, I settle into a new school. I know our living arrangements are temporary, so I purposely stay quiet and alone. Despite my best efforts not to, I love my new school and make lots of friends. Unfortunately, I'm behind in my classes, especially math and French. I stay after school several days a week for unrealistic tutoring. Nothing will help the Grand Canyon–sized brain gaps from five years of gypsy-esque living and, as my new math teacher put it, "The lack of Louisiana learning standards."

My inadequate education is the least of my problems. Eric, Jenny, and I are thankful for the luxuries of proper food and supervision, yet a life with basic needs isn't always the happiest. Our overcautious grandmother won't let us go outside unless she is with us. I stare out my bedroom window at the concrete and the little I can see of the well-kept trailer park. Stuck in a mobile tin can, we have the pleasure of hanging out with our grandmother's husband, Walter, the kid-hating asshole.

The kitchen is off-limits except for food consumption. Living room access requires stringent adherence to rules and regulations. In order to be present in the same room as Walter, we must be absolutely quiet and literally do nothing and more of nothing—no television, no talking, and certainly no laughing. Well, we can watch the news, westerns, and boxing with Walter, as long as we stay still and quiet. And God forbid we breathe too loudly when he's reading the newspaper. Violations mean banishment to the hallway or to our rooms, where life continues in silence or whispered voices. I swear Eric does shit just to get Walter going like a tea kettle.

Our only change of scenery occurs when our grandmother makes us go to church. We've gone to at least a dozen different churches with her, so I'm over searching for Jesus in a new building. For a woman who cycles through husbands like she does churches, my grandmother has a lot of nerve. I make one phone call to a football player named Jeremy, and she forbids me from talking on the phone. I've had it up to my eyeballs with being smothered to death, so I begin operation rebellion. I'm openly uncooperative, defy Walter's ridiculous rules, and frequently curse and slam doors when she and Walter give me grief about it.

⋏

May finally rolls around, and we return to Louisiana for Mother's court date. On the witness stand, I recount how poor we were, how there wasn't enough money for dog food, and how we fed them when we could. The whole time, Mother looks at me like she hopes I don't betray our family by telling the whole truth and nothing but the truth, so help her God. She pays a fine and has to find a new place for us to live, because we can't pay the rent.

Jenny returns to Texas with our grandmother. Mother and Eric move in with our cousin Rachel and her family. I move in with Stella so I can finish my freshman year at our original high school. Three weeks later, I begin the summer of 1993 by joining Mother and Eric. Shortly after, a slumber party at Chloe's house forever alters my existence.

CHAPTER 8

BOYS

"They're coming over!" Iris shrieks after she hangs up the phone in Chloe's room.

I reluctantly turn down the television. "Who?" I yell from the living room. "Who?" I yell again, feeling like an owl, but I get no response. I look over at Amber, and we both move from the couch to Chloe's room, but we end up in the bathroom instead.

Taller than all of us, Amber stands beside me in the doorway and places her elbow gently on my shoulder. Iris has a big smile on her face and a curling iron in one hand as she fixes her dark blond hair. Chloe explains, "Nick and his two friends are stopping by on their way home from the movies."

"I thought your mom said "no boys," I remind Chloe and watch as she puts on a fresh coat of mascara. This little bathroom has one small mirror, which I suspect the three of them will soon attempt to use all at once.

"She won't be back till around three, after the bar closes," Chloe responds, with a mischievous smile that reveals her braces.

I imagine Mother's car suddenly pulling into the driveway and say, "It's bad enough your mom left. My mom will kill me if she ever finds out."

"How's she gonna know?" Chloe asks, to which I have no reply.

"I'm surprised she even let you come in the first place," Iris says to me while teasing her bangs to their usual perfection.

"You and me both," I say quietly. *It's all about timing. She was in a good mood that day.*

Chloe stops with her mascara wand in the air and looks at me. "It's not like you lied to her. I didn't know my mom was going out either."

Amber and I look at each other and shrug our shoulders. With a sideways glance in the mirror, Iris informs us that our guests will be here in fifteen minutes. Amber disappears into Chloe's room and reappears in nicer clothes. I stand in the bathroom doorway and watch them fuss about until the smell of Aqua Net hairspray chases me away.

When I sit on Chloe's bed, Amber finally notices my lack of urgency and asks, "You're not getting dressed?"

I sigh and reply, "What's the point?"

Chloe walks in and searches the nightstand and dresser for her new tube of red lipstick. I admire her curly red hair until she gives me a funny look and says, "You're still wearing that? Get dressed!"

I look down at myself. "I guess not," I mumble and grab my bag.

The four of us pile into the bathroom.

Makeup is all over the place, and a cooling curling iron balances on the back of the toilet. My long hair is once again out of control. Amber tells me that I look fine and leaves me alone to fight with it. I look in the mirror and put down the brush. *Ugh. Oh well. And there's the doorbell. Doesn't matter anyway. Not meeting the man of my dreams here.*

My eyes roll as I throw my makeup and hairbrush into my bag and chuck it in Chloe's room. I rush to the couch to join Chloe's and Amber's attempts to look casual.

"What's wrong?" asks Chloe.

"Nothing," I reply and try to neutralize my face. *Indifference, not hostility.*

Leading her man by the hand, Iris strolls past the kitchen and into the living room area. Nick looks pretty much the same as I remember from junior high. Chloe, Amber, and I stand to greet him. Nick gives me a big hug and says, "Long time no see." When we let go, his hand returns home and wraps around Iris's fingers.

"Yeah, it's been a few years," I say, with my attention drawn to the two strangers who linger behind him—one is taller than the other and smoking a cigarette.

Nick begins introductions, "Oh, sorry. These are my friends Marcus and John."

Marcus smiles, exchanges pleasantries, and shakes our hands. *Medium build. Black hair. Not bad looking. What am I saying?*

I look at John, who shakes our hands with little enthusiasm. *Trouble. White T-shirt. Blue jeans. Tall and lean. Broad shoulders. Blond hair. Blue eyes. No, no, no! Warning! Disaster! Trouble.*

The boys pull up chairs from the kitchen table. Nick and I catch up. Chloe explains that it's her sixteenth birthday. Iris calls her an old lady, because the rest of us are fifteen. Marcus and Nick discuss the movie.

John remains silent for the most part. I ask him a few questions, to which he responds with clipped answers. *Okay then.* I turn to Marcus. He asks me several questions that I reluctantly answer with a polite smile. I catch my eyes wandering over to John, mostly because he's directly across from me, which is the lie they keep telling me every time they glance at his face. *He's not saying much. So serious…yet his eyes don't match the "not interested" look on his face.*

Like a good hostess, Chloe offers them drinks, and everyone goes into the kitchen. Ice tinkles into glasses, and cans of Dr. Pepper are passed out. I go to take a sip despite the foam… *and there exit Iris and Nick into Chloe's room. Sneaky.*

Small talk quickly becomes awkward silence. Chloe and Amber keep looking at me. *This is ridiculous. I'm not even interested. When did I become the one in charge? When the love birds bailed. Fine.* I bombard our guests with questions.

⋏

An eternity passes—ten minutes, actually—before Iris and Nick come back into the living room. Iris walks right up to me as I'm about to answer a question from Marcus and says, "I need to talk to you." I look up at her, and she continues with emphasis, "Alone."

"Okay?" I reply and excuse myself. I follow her into Chloe's room, and she shuts the door. We sit on the bed. *Let me guess, this will be something about sex. I'm not sure what she expects me to…*

She begins, "Okay. Here's the deal. I want Nick to stay awhile, but they're supposed to be on their way home. John's driving his mom's pickup truck, and Nick says that if, maybe, you're interested in one of the guys, then they can stay longer."

"What?" I say and shake my head on the way to the door.

"Come on. You owe me."

I hesitate to twist the knob. "Wait a minute. What do you mean, I owe you?"

"You owe me for Ted and the skating rink."

"What? Oh. Dammit." I return to my spot on the bed. *I knew that shit would come back to haunt me.*

"Well?" she pleads.

I debate my options and remind her, "You know I'm not interested in dating anyone. Ever."

She grabs my hand and implores, with puppy dog eyes, "Please?"

I think about her occupying Ben so I could hang out with Ted more, and I sigh. "Fine. But never again."

"Yes!" she exclaims and gives me a hug.

"What exactly do you want me to do?" I ask.

"Just seem interested, flirt, whatever."

Is that what I told her? "With which one?" I say apathetically.

"Which one do you like?"

"I don't."

With exasperation, she says, "You know what I mean."

"I don't know."

"Who's cuter?"

"John," I admit. *But he's trouble.*

"That's Nick's best friend."

"Great," I say and resist the urge to roll my eyes. "He looks like trouble."

"Well, Marcus then."

And what the hell am I supposed to do to accomplish this? I don't do this kind of thing. Improvise? I stare at Chloe's digital clock on the nightstand, and the little red lines change by one number. "I guess… Marcus it is."

Iris cheers, "Yay!" and bolts for the door. Nick is all smug on the other side. As we pass each other in the doorway, he says, "Thanks."

"Yeah, yeah," I reply and tuck my hair behind my ears. The door shuts behind me.

Marcus and John are deep in conversation at the end of the kitchen counter. Chloe and Amber are turned around on the couch, facing them. As I move closer to the boys, Marcus gives me a big smile. I smile back and stop between them. I turn toward John, who gives me this "yes?" expression. The tiny smile is quite a change from the scowl. Turning back toward Marcus, I say, "Let's go outside for a walk."

One says, "Okay, yeah," in unison with the other saying, "Cool."

They both turn to walk to the door, but I link my arm with Marcus's and say, "So you and I can talk." I glance over at John, who stops and says, "Oh," with a frown.

Chloe asks, "Where are they going?"

As I close the door, my eyes meet John's, and he answers, "For a walk."

CHAPTER 9

DARKNESS

Outside is surprisingly warm and not deathly hot, buttery humid for the end of July. The moonless sky leaves everything dark, and so are most of the houses lined up on both sides of the street. I imagine the neighbors are off in dreamland or curled up with the ten o'clock news. There are only two streetlights—one uselessly far down at the end of the road, and the other bright and annoying in the corner of Chloe's backyard. The latter makes the front side of her house a deep, dark, shadowy place.

Marcus and I mosey up and down the narrow street. He is friendly and a gentleman, but our stilted conversation is mostly small talk. A car's bright lights go around us. When more approach, we step off the street into the grass and continue our walk counterclockwise around the house.

"It is really dark on this side," I comment.

"Especially with that light blinding you," he says, finishing my thought.

We take a wide curve through the front yard to stay in the path of light. On our second revolution, we pass the corner of the house where the dark and light meet. My words falter as I try to rationalize the sight of one orange firefly. I jump when I realize the little glow in the dark is a person smoking a cigarette. "Who is…?" I ask, but Marcus interrupts me with, "It's just John." He hooks his arm with mine, and we continue on our way. I use one hand to emphasize where I left off.

Next thing I know, John walks toward us, near the spot we last saw him. He almost collides with us, but he swerves at the last second, muttering to himself.

"What is his problem?" I ask my new friend.

Marcus replies, "My guess is that he wants to leave."

I look at Chloe's window. *Good. I don't know how much longer I can keep this up.*

About halfway around the darkest part of the yard, Marcus begins to guide us out of the light's path and toward the house. "Where are you going? Hello. Can't see," I say.

"I want to show you something."

"Ha, ha. Very funny." I correct course because I know we are in enormous bush territory. Marcus turns us back around and maneuvers deeper into the darkness.

All amusement gone, I say, "Seriously? What are you doing? It's too dark." I attempt to pull my arm away, but Marcus twirls me around, and I find myself up against the house. "Ew, spider webs," I say as I feel them on my arms.

Distracted by the real possibility of spiders crawling on me, I don't notice the one in my face. Marcus tries to kiss me. "Whoa!" I say, with a quick turn of my head, and all he gets is cheek. "What the hell are you doing?" I nudge him back with my hands on his chest.

He pushes me back up against the house with his body and nuzzles into my ear, "Trying to get to know you better."

This is really happening. Gentleman, my ass! "Uh, no! I think it's time to go back inside!" I push and try to move left and right. He has me pinned and proceeds to slobber down my neck. At my collarbone, he asks, "What? You don't want to have a little fun?"

"Not this kind of fun! I'm not that type of girl!" I pointlessly squirm left and right.

"Come on…you'll like it," he says, with roaming hands.

Pissed, I demand, "Stop right now!" My hands deflect most of his rough advances, but then he grabs my forearm.

CHAPTER 10

LIGHT

"Marcus, leave the girl alone. She said no," orders an annoyed voice from the darkness in front of me. I see an orange glow brighten and float closer. Relief floods over the roar in my ears. I watch the tiny light like a moth and wait for Marcus to let go of my arm. He doesn't. I try to move to my right, away from them both.

"Mind your own goddamn business, John!" Marcus yells over his shoulder and resumes being an ass.

Great. Guess I'll handle this myself. "Get the *fuck* off me!" I shout and shove Marcus far enough away to get my knee up.

"Marcus! Let. Her. Go," growls the voice.

Marcus and I instantly freeze. *Shit just got real scary. They're going to fight, and there's going to be blood and murder and police and…shit, my mother, 'cause this asshole can't keep…*

Marcus releases my arm and storms off with a shout. "This is bullshit! I didn't want to come to this fucking party anyway!"

My ears track his movements. I hear more complaints followed by a loud "fuck." I open my eyes to see Marcus waving his arms. *Ha! Ran into the bushes. Serves him right!*

"You okay?" John asks with a gentle voice.

My brain snaps to full attention. I let out a held breath of panic and breathe in anger. "Yeah. I'm fine," I answer and adjust my shirt and dust myself off. I wipe my cheek, ear, and neck with my T-shirt. "Gross," I say, disgusted.

"Are you sure?" he asks, and when that orange glow brightens, I realize he's about five feet to my left.

I grumble, "Yeah. I'll live." My fingers try to work fast through my tousled hair.

"Good," he says and walks away toward the light of the backyard.

I attempt to follow and find vocabulary. All I can get out is, "Your friend is a real asshole!"

He abruptly halts and replies, "True."

I take a few steps closer. "Thanks for…"

Half turning, he says, "Don't mention it," and flicks what's left of the cigarette toward the house. I watch it arc into the darkness and disappear. I look back to see him walk away into the light.

"Wait." I try to catch up. "You're John, right?"

He stops and blows out a breath. Turning completely around this time, he says, "I thought you liked him."

The light behind him is bright, and I can only see his silhouette. With renewed anger, I say, "I did, but I met the guy like five minutes ago. Doesn't mean he gets to maul me like a bear. Stupid jerk was about to get a knee to the balls."

He chuckles. "Maybe Marcus should be the one thanking me."

My anger evaporates. *So, Mr. Serious has a sense of humor.*

He doesn't say anything more, and I stare back, which is pointless, because the light keeps his face obscured. I glance around us. The chirp, chirp, chirping symphony of crickets makes me smile. *Why am I so tired all of a sudden?* I frown and run a hand down my neck to make sure it's dry.

The continued silence drives me bananas, so I move closer and stop inside his shadow. With eyes on my feet, I confess, "Look. To be honest, I was only talking to him so y'all would stay, and Iris could spend time with Nick." *Why am I telling him this?* I look up and realize that he towers over me by more than a foot. He tilts his head to the side. I sigh and explain, "I owed her a favor." I tuck my hair behind my ears and wait for him to speak.

"Yes, I'm John. Without the *h*. Short for Jonathan. And you're Tina."

"Yes. Actually, my name is Constantina, but everyone calls me Tina."

I step up beside him and can see his handsome face in the light. We start a slow walk.

"That's a beautiful name," he says.

"Thanks. I'm named after my grandmother."

After a few more steps, he stops, turns to me, and says, "Just to make it clear, I'm not interested in starting a relationship or having a girlfriend."

"Perfect, Jon without the *h*, 'cause I have no interest in having a boyfriend."

CHAPTER 11

HANDS

Jon nonchalantly picks cobwebs out of my hair as we wander around the backyard and absorb each other's lives. So many things… our ages, schools, families, where we live, how we met our best friends.

He's surprised that I knew Nick before Iris did. I explain, "I lived in Grant Parish for a year. Nick and I used to ride the same bus when I was in junior high. He sat with me because I apparently had big boobs for a seventh grader. Iris shared that piece of information with me, to Nick's mortification."

Laughing, Jon says, "That's sounds like Nick all right."

I assumed wrong when we were first introduced. Not another cute jerk that's full of himself. Charming, genuine, talkative. Has a great laugh. I don't have to try with him. Like recognizing an old and dearest friend. I can see why Nick considers him a best friend. I like him. Even like like him. Maybe I was too hasty about my relationship status. Never expected to meet someone like him. Oh well, he's not interested in a girlfriend. Too bad.

Our nonstop conversation and banter are interrupted by the slam of the house door followed by the truck door. "Maybe we should go inside," I suggest.

"Yeah, good idea," he says, looking at the truck.

Our long shadows move through the grass in front of us until the outside house light unexpectedly brightens the driveway. When I open the door to go in, I glance to see what has Jon's attention and find Marcus glaring at us from inside the pickup truck.

I stop and glare right back. "That motherfucker," I say and take a step toward the truck.

Jon puts his hand on my back and guides me into the house. Before he shuts the door between us, he says in a serious tone, "Go inside. I'll handle him."

I enter the kitchen and stop at the table. Iris, Nick, Chloe, and Amber come up off the couch.

"What the hell happened?" Iris begins as she stops in front of me.

Amber steps beside her and says, "You were gone for a long time."

"Why did Marcus come in all pissed?" Chloe adds, followed by Nick asking, "Where's Jon?"

So many questions. Good thing I wasn't dead out there. They surround me and wait for an explanation. Iris picks a web from my hair with a "what the hell is this?" face. My legs ache from all the outdoor activities, so I sit, and everyone picks a chair except for Nick, who remains standing between Iris and me.

I explain, "Well, Marcus was all nice until he decided to corner me in the dark up against the house. Jon stopped him, and Marcus stormed off."

In unison, the girls gasp, and Nick says, with a hand in the air, "What the fuck, Marcus?"

Not knowing what else to tell them, I look down at my hands and notice a thumbprint-sized bruise on my inner forearm below my wrist. I hide my hands under the table and say, "I've been talking to Jon ever since."

Chloe says, "Well, that explains Marcus."

"Are you all right?" Amber asks.

"Yes," I say. "Thanks to Jon."

Everyone's eyes move behind me as Jon walks into the room. "Yes?" he says to them and then gives me a little smile.

I stand up to face him. "What happened?" I question.

"Nothing to worry about," he tells me and then says to Nick, "Marcus is being a dick, among other things."

They continue talking, but I can't follow. I feel Amber's fingers move my arm around. "You've got a bruise on your arm," she says and lets me go when I look down at her.

I cover it with a hand and quietly say to her, "I know."

Jon stops midsentence. He looks at my face and then down at my arm. I reluctantly show him. "He bruised you," he says and takes my wrist with a warm hand. His thumb brushes the mark. Completely preoccupied, I say, "I've had worse."

Confusion tempers the anger on his face. I see the question forming and scramble for a lie. All are interrupted by the long and loud bellow of the truck horn. He releases me. Iris and Chloe maneuver in to take a look.

"We've gotta go," Jon says to Nick.

I frown, and Iris says, "Dammit."

The horn blows again. I glare at the door and the noise on the other side. *Does Chloe have a baseball bat?* Meanwhile, there's some kind of discussion behind me about paper with Amber and something about Nick being right back. Iris follows Nick out the door anyway.

Chloe, still standing next to me, yells after them, "Tell that asshole to quit blowing that goddamn horn at one thirty in the morning! My neighbors are gonna call the cops!" She then turns me around, moves my hair out of the way, and looks at the back of my black shirt. "You're covered in cobwebs," she says.

I change clothes in her room, and I'm back in the bathroom with my brush. In the middle of cursing at the last of the webs, I notice Jon's amused face in the mirror. My cheeks catch fire as I rotate toward the open doorway.

He hands me a piece of paper. I unfold it to see his full name and phone number. I stammer, "I thought…I thought you didn't…"

He looks at me for a long moment and says, with a half smile, "Well, I wasn't expecting to meet you." My face continues to burn. He grins and says, "I have to go."

"Wait. Give me like two minutes, and I'll say goodbye."

"Two minutes," he nods and walks away.

I shut the door. I have to pee so badly.

⋏

As I wash my hands, the door opens, and Chloe's curls flash in and out like red lightning.

And now I have chocolate syrup in my hair. "Goddamn it, Chloe! What the actual fuck?" I yell and slam the door.

Apparently, while I was busy in the bathroom, my good old pals decided it was time to throw shit at each other. With a big glob of soap, I attempt damage control once again.

I hear someone outside the door, to whom I yell, "Bitches! Do not throw any more food at me!" *I would be dead if I threw food around my mother's perfectly cleaned house.* The door opens anyway because the lock is broken, and Iris enters, hand raised, complete with an egg. I give her a murderous look. She pulls up short and says, "What the hell is wrong with you?"

"I have to say goodbye…to Jon," I answer, saying the last part quietly.

"What do you mean you have to say goodbye to Jon?"

Amber's head sneaks in from behind her to say that they're leaving now. In a panic, I wash faster. Amber runs off, and the house shakes as she and Chloe jump around and scream at each other. *I give up on my hair and this never-ending parade of bubbles.* I give Iris a sheepish glance and grab a towel from a cabinet.

"You like him? I thought you weren't 'interested in anyone ever,'" she says, mimicking my voice at the last part.

"We started talking and…" I put the towel on the back of the toilet and hand her the paper from my pocket. I attempt to comb wet tangles.

Iris's face lights up. "He gave you his number!"

Chloe appears behind her to lob an egg at me. Iris stops her with an arm across the doorway and quickly says, "She has to say goodbye to Jon!"

Chloe's arm lowers a bit. "What? Say goodbye to Jon? What are you talking about?"

Aye. So many questions this evening. I grab the note from Iris, and they both move to the side. When I pass through the kitchen, I give Amber the stink eye and a stern "don't even think about it" warning.

"We're just playing around," she says as I shut the front door.

⋏

Jon stands alone with his back against the front of the pickup truck. Nick sits on the passenger side. He looks pleased as punch and gives me a wink. Marcus sits beside him in the middle with crossed arms and a frowny face turned toward the driver's side window.

"Sorry I took forever. Everyone started throwing food. I got chocolate syrup in my hair," I explain and point to the top of the wet chunk.

"It's okay," he says and takes my raised hand, which is so small compared to his. He smiles and holds out his other hand for my free one.

Oh, why not? I really do like him.

He holds my hands and rubs his thumbs across my knuckles. His fingers are slightly rough. "Oh," I say and let go, reacting more to his touch than the sudden darkness of the outside house light disappearing. *Those little she-devils!*

I can still see his face, thanks to that not-so-annoying backyard light, and he nods toward it. I take his hand this time and guide us to about fifty feet from the truck. When we stop, I turn my back to the light so I can still see his face.

"So," he starts and looks at our still-joined hands. "You're going to call me, right…even though you're not interested in a boyfriend?"

I don't answer. Worry replaces his crooked grin. "I suppose," I say indifferently and look around us. He drops my hand. "Yes, I'll call you," I say, laughing, and push my arm into his.

"Funny," he says and pushes back.

We remain close, and I feel the warmth of his body. *He smells so good. Some type of cologne. Wonder what it is?*

"So, Alan, huh?" I ask, in reference to his note.

He smiles in confirmation and asks, "And you?"

"Marie."

He pronounces my full name and looks over my face. "Beautiful," he says, and I smile as hollow places in my bones fill with that one word. Like he suddenly remembers, he glances over his shoulder to the truck and says, "I have stuff to do in the morning, so call me after one."

I tell him that I will. "Wait, I can't. We're going to Stuart's Lake in the afternoon. I can call you after, when I get home. Or you know…you should come with." *He'll get to see me in my bathing suit. That should be fun.*

He frowns. "No way I can go now. My mom's gonna be pissed that I'm back so late. I doubt she'll let me have her truck tomorrow. I'll try to get another ride, but no promises."

Motionless silence ticks by until his pale eyes flicker down to my mouth twice.

Shit! I take two steps back, but then he asks, "Can I kiss you?"

And there he goes asking permission. Hmm…decisions, decisions. "Just don't paw me to death. I've had quite enough of that for the evening."

"No hands. I swear," he says and puts them behind his back.

"Fine then."

We step closer to each other, and he leans down. I close my eyes. Ever so gently, he places an innocent kiss upon my lips, and I instantly know he's different from the few boys I've kissed before. My whole body electrifies from my lips down to my toes and out the ends of my hair, as if I've been an inanimate object my whole existence, and I've suddenly come to life.

Up on tippy-toes as far as possible, I wrap my arms around his neck. "*Mmm*," he purrs, and our mouths open a tiny bit as my fingers play through his short hair.

The slow kiss ends with my feet firmly on the ground. My heart does jumping jacks and tries to outdo my hot face. Jon whispers in my ear, "I thought we agreed no hands?"

I promptly drop them to my sides and say with a grin, "I didn't say anything about my hands."

He laughs, grabs my shoulders, and turns us around, with me facing the light. "I love that you blush," he tells me. I cover my face with my hands. "It's cute," he says, taking them away.

"Glad I could amuse you," I retort and cross my eyes.

"You silly girl," he laughs and shakes his head. Looking past me to the truck, he remembers again. "I've really got to go this time."

We walk to the front door with fingers entwined. When we hug goodbye, he says, "Good night, Constantina," to which I respond, "Good night, Jonathan."

I wave as the truck pulls out of the driveway, and I open the door to find three mother hens standing in a row. "Well?" they ask in unison.

All night long. I've never been asked so many questions in my life. I answer, "Well, we like each other," and receive two surprised responses of "really?" I look at Iris and gesture toward the other two. Iris shakes her head and says, "You explain."

On our way to the couch, I hand the folded paper to Chloe. "That's why you had to say goodbye," she says with a grin. "Yes, explain."

"He did give you his number," Amber confirms after she takes the paper from Chloe.

Before I can even sit down, Iris asks sweetly, with raised eyebrows, "Did you say goodbye?"

"Yes…and he kissed me," I say matter-of-factly to her.

Amber and Chloe squeal, "He kissed you!"

A smiling Iris nods her head like she knows something I don't.

Chloe continues, "Explain already!"

"Well…" I start.

"I thought you weren't interested in anyone ever," Amber interrupts and hands me the note.

"True," I reply.

CHAPTER 12

SMITTEN

Jon and I talk on the phone for at least an hour every day. We never run out of things to say as we talk about our childhoods, interests, parents, past relationships, and all the infinite details that make us who we are. Depending on his work schedule, we eat meals together over the phone.

Carefully timed negotiations land me at Iris's house every weekend. We meet up with our boyfriends at the local hangout. Jon likes to play pool, but I love to roller-skate and insist on doing so even without him.

"Come here, woman!" he says and fails to grab me when I skate around the bend, just out of reach. "You know we don't have very long together. Come play some pool with me."

"Fine. Ruin my fun," I tease and skate back to him with a kiss. When I let go, his smile is missing. I search his expressionless face and watch a flash of anger wither into sadness. "What's wrong?" I question.

He stares past me. "Just thinking about if another guy was kissing you instead of me."

"What? Why would you think something like that?"

He looks down at my feet then back up to my face. "It's weird. You're really tall in those skates," he says with a laugh.

"Want me to leave them on?" I ask as we move toward a bench.

"Nope. I prefer you just the way you are."

After he helps me put on my shoes, we join Iris and Nick at a pool table. The boys need to finish their game. Even though Iris already taught me how to play, I feign ignorance and give her a wink. She tries not to laugh as Jon shows me how to properly hold the stick. I just want to get close. Jon grins at Nick when we ready the next shot. With the exception of kickball, sports are not my forte, but I manage to knock the ball into a corner pocket.

When we finish, Iris challenges them to a game—girls versus boys. Jon takes it easy on us and gives me pointers until I sink three balls in a row.

Nick says to Jon, "I think someone was yanking your chain."

Iris and I crack up laughing at Jon's face. "You little minx!" he says and grabs me.

Between the pokes to my ribs and the resulting squirms and laughter, I say, "Hey, I never said I didn't know how to play. You just assumed, and I went along with it."

Jon single-handedly finishes the game, and we begin another. I tell him that I'm no match for Iris, and sometimes I get lucky, but I'm on his team anyway. After he breaks, sending the balls flying and sinking a solid, he checks his wristwatch. "I'll be right back," he says and walks toward the glass doors at the front entrance. I see Marcus on the other side in the hallway.

"What the hell is he doing here?" I ask Nick, who responds, "He wants to apologize to you so we can all be friends again."

Iris says, "He should be apologizing for being a jackass."

"I have nothing nice to say to him," I tell Nick and turn my attention back to the game, but Nick says, "Oh, he's definitely sorry, especially after the fight with Jon. He's still sporting a shiner."

I look at Nick and then back at the front doors. Jon motions me over, but I shake my head. He leaves Marcus at the entrance and walks right up to me. Before he can get a word out, I say, "Nope. I have nothing to say to that asshole. I don't care if he does apologize."

"Tina, he wants to make peace with you and apologize for what he did." He looks at Nick and continues, "We've known him for almost our entire lives, and he's serious. He learned his lesson. I made sure of that."

"Did you really get into a fight?"

"Go see for yourself."

"Fine," I say with a sigh, "but you're going with me."

"Of course," he says.

⚚

Marcus is too busy with shifty feet and fidgety hands to notice me in the hallway. Jon gives me a reassuring nod from his post on the other side of the closed door. "What do you want, Marcus?" I ask, with crossed arms, and stop a good three feet away from him.

"I...uh, thanks for agreeing to talk to me," he says, with an unsure smile.

"Well, you can thank your friends for that," I say, not giving one inch of sympathy.

"I just wanted to make things right and apologize for the way I treated you. I had no right to do what I did. I know it was wrong. I scared and hurt you, and I'm sorry for all of it."

I don't say anything as I focus on his face and see the remnants of a black eye. "Are you sincere, or are you just trying to get in good with your friends?"

"Oh, no, I'm sincere. I'm not a bad a person, Tina. I just made a mistake that won't ever happen again."

"With just me or anyone else for the rest of your life?"

"Both. I'll be a perfect gentleman from now on. I promise."

"I don't know, Marcus. I'm having a little trouble trusting your word."

"I know, but if you give me a chance to prove it, we can be friends, and you'll see."

I glance over at Jon, who looks hopeful. "Alright, Marcus, I'll forgive you, but you better not get one hair out of line, or I'll have Jon kick your ass again."

"I would expect nothing less," he says with relief and a smile. He goes to give me a hug but changes his mind and shakes my hand instead. "I've got to go," he says and releases my hand. "My ride went to get gas and will be right back to get me. I'll see you next time."

"See you later," I say and return to Jon, who holds the door open for me.

"How did it go?" he asks.

"He seemed sincere, so I forgave him," I reply, to which I receive a hug, a kiss, and a "thank you" in return. "What time is it?" I ask and grab his arm to look at his watch. "Shit! It's already four o'clock. My mother said she'd be here at three thirty. She's going to kill me if she's been waiting all this time."

I say a hasty goodbye to our friends, but Jon stops before the glass doors and says, "Nick has my lighter. Don't leave without me."

"No promises," I call over my shoulder as I exit and sprint down the long hallway to the building entryway.

※

I burst out the door to find Marcus seated on the sidewalk. He hasn't seen a blond woman in a blue two-door car. My eyes dart back and forth over the parking lot twice before I ask him, "What happened to your ride?"

"I don't know. Sometimes five minutes turns into half an hour."

"Yeah, I know how that is. My mom said she'd be here at three thirty. I could be waiting out here till five."

"Well, we can keep each other company," he says. After I make myself comfortable on the ground next to him, he looks toward the doors and asks, "Where's Jon?"

"Oh, he's tracking down his lighter. He's apparently the only one who has one, so there's no telling where it is."

"You don't smoke?"

"No. Tried it few times, but it was blah, not worth getting addicted to. Now candy bars on the other hand, that's my problem."

He laughs and says, "Thank you, Tina."

"For what?"

"You're very kind. Jon said so and said that if I apologized, you'd forgive me."

"He did now, did he?"

"Yes. Not that I had much of a choice with him being in love with you and us going to be together all the time…oh, shit! I didn't mean to say that!"

"Wait, what? Did you just say what I think you said?"

"No. Yes. Shit. He's gonna kill me."

"He's in love with me?"

"I'm not saying another word."

"Marcus! Spill!"

"Ok, yes. You're all he thinks about and talks about, and he dreams about you, and frankly, we're all sick of it. No offense. Just please don't tell Jon…" He stops with wide eyes.

Jon exits the door behind me with an unlit cigarette between his fingers and says, "Don't tell me what?"

Marcus and I hop to our feet. Right on cue, Marcus's ride pulls up, he jumps in with a "bye," and off he goes.

Jon stands right in front of me, but I'm all zippy lippy and shrug my shoulders. He says, "So five minutes later, you and Marcus are best friends and keeping secrets."

"Hey, you're the one that wanted me to forgive him, so now we're friends, and friends keep secrets."

"Okay. What is it? What is it I'm not supposed to know?" he says, not giving up.

I answer with an annoyed face, "Oh, you know already. It's just that I know now."

He doesn't say anything else, and I watch his playful demeanor vanish. "What do you mean?" he asks.

"I'll tell you if you answer me one question," I continue with attitude, despite the laughter about to spill out.

"Go ahead," he says.

"Do you love me?" I ask, to which he opens his mouth but nothing comes out. "Jonathan, are you blushing?" I giggle as his face turns a pale shade of pink.

"Did Marcus tell you that?" he asks, running a hand through his hair.

"In so many words, by accident, but I dragged it out of him, so don't be mad at him," I explain. He remains silent, as if he's unsure how to respond. I turn away from him and say, "Well, if you do or you don't, either way…"

Suddenly, his hands are on both sides of my face. "Yes. I love you," he says and when my mouth drops open, he kisses me.

Two minutes later, a car horn separates us.

"I'll call you tonight, and we can finish this…conversation," he tells me and waves at Mother. To my utter shock, she smiles and waves back.

From inside the car, I watch Jon in the side mirror as Mother drives away. *Will we even make it out of the parking lot?* I prepare for the onslaught.

"So, who was that?" she asks.

"That's Jonathan," I answer.

"And is he your boyfriend?"

"Yes, ma'am."

"He's handsome."

"Yes, ma'am. I think so."

"How'd you meet?"

"At a birthday party."

"When did this happen?"

"At Chloe's party, the day after the slumber party. It was coed like my fourteenth birthday party. That's how we met," I lie.

"Well, lucky you," she says.

CHAPTER 13

JACKIE

I **revel in freedom** when Aunt Jackie kidnaps me on weekends and holidays. Originally a friend of Jim's, she has been in and out of my life ever since the big brawl with Mother.

On our way to her house, we often grab movies from Blockbuster and food from the drive-through at Taco Bell. From time to time, we watch meteor showers, play Dungeons and Dragons, and hang out with her gay friends. Most of the time, we stay up all night, listen to music, and talk. No subject is taboo. Jackie is everything Mother is supposed to be—a trustworthy mentor and best friend.

Unfortunately, my oppressor often banishes Jackie from my life out of jealousy or the need to punish me. Jackie and I must exceed expectations in the ass-kissing department. Lots of placating and groveling. A few hours to several months later, Jackie returns from exile and spends time with Mother. When I get a nod or a wink from Jackie, I know there's a high chance I will escape. Then, like Mary Poppins, except in a Honda Civic, she whisks me away for fun and adventure. A spoonful of Jackie's kindness always helps the insanity go down.

⊥

"That was Jon!" I shout.

"Are you sure?" Jackie asks and checks her mirrors.

"Yes! Absolutely! U-turn! U-turn!"

"Okay! Okay!"

We U-turn twice, and I roll down my window as we pull along beside him. Jackie stops the car. He looks at us with alarm and then surprise. "Hi!" he says. "What are you doing out here?"

"Hi!" I giggle. "We are on our way home. Where ya going?"

"To Nick's house. I thought you were with…this must be Aunt Jackie." They introduce themselves and shake hands.

"Where exactly do you live?" I ask him.

He points to the house across the street. I stifle a laugh as Jackie gives me a face and says to him, "I live down the next road."

"You've been right here. All this time," he says to me and takes my hand. Our fingers entwine.

"Seems so," I say, thinking the same thing.

Jackie says, "Hate to cut this short, but…"

Jon and I look behind us and see cars coming up fast. In unison, we say, "Call me later."

As Jackie drives away, she says, "Hmm…" and as soon as we enter her house, the two of us formulate a plan.

⊥

The night before Jon comes over, I search for a movie we can watch together. I can't find anything good, despite the never-ending rows of VHS tapes that line the entertainment center shelves. Jackie tells me to play what's in the VCR. The remote control is nowhere to be found, so I sit directly in front of her thirty-inch television to reach the play button on the VCR. The tape plays, and I'm confused. "Jackie, what am I looking at?"

She laughs and asks, "You don't know what's happening?"

"I don't...I don't even know what this is...and that's a penis...and apparently a vagina."

The angle seems sideways, and the perspective is extremely close. I've never seen the two put together, much less so graphically, with thrusting and grunting. The video is fuzzy and old, like something from the 1970s.

"Well, you're still a virgin for sure."

"You could have just asked," I say, beet red.

"Well, now that you know what sex is, what do you think?"

"It looks...complicated...and gross."

She cracks up laughing. "Well, maybe this wasn't the best example to start off with. I have more..." she says, digging around a stack of tapes.

"No, that's okay, Jackie. I've got the gist of it."

"Sex doesn't start off like that. You caught more of the middle...or actually the end."

"I got it, Jackie," I say, backing away, and peel my eyes off the TV.

Jackie laughs again, turns off the VCR, and asks, "Any questions?"

"Does it hurt the first time?"

"Well, yes, but not for long. If the guy is good and knows what he's doing, he'll be careful and gentle, and you won't even remember. I mean, you'll be sore for a day or so afterwards. Just make sure he has a condom."

"Yes, I will, but what's a condom?" After she explains what it is, how it's applied, and what it prevents, I say, "Thanks for the advice, but I wasn't planning on going that far."

"Well, from what you've told me, Jon's charming. Things happen. I want you to be prepared."

"Thank you," I say, grateful to finally have "the talk" with an adult. I never learned anything at school beyond random classmates getting pregnant and a fifth-grade video about periods, boobs, pimples, and body hair. All Mother told me was that boys only want one thing and not to give it to them, otherwise I'll be a slut.

"Ya know, there are other things you could do," Jackie says.

"What do you mean?"

"Like hand jobs and blow jobs."

"Okay? Explain, please," I say.

"You really haven't done anything with him."

"We've only kissed and held hands."

"With tongue?"

"Yes, Jackie, I've got the kissing part down."

She says, "Just making sure," and launches into an explanation of this job business.

CHAPTER 14

MOVIES

Our little trio laughs at the misadventures of Ash in *Army of Darkness*. Jackie is on the love seat, and Jon and I are on the floor, with his back against the empty side. I sit in front of him with my back against his chest and his legs on either side of me.

I can't fully concentrate on the movie. Jon's fingers run non-stop through the ends of my hair, and every once in a while, he leans down and kisses the side of my neck. Each time Jackie exits the room to smoke a cigarette or use the bathroom, Jon and I kiss until we hear her approach.

About halfway through the movie, she presses pause, stands, and says, "I'm going downstairs to make some popcorn, so if you guys want to make out some more, I'll be gone for at least six minutes."

After she goes downstairs, and before we resume kissing, Jon says, with a chuckle and shake of his head, "I like your Aunt Jackie," to which I reply, "See, I told you."

The second evening, Jackie makes dinner, and the three of us eat at the kitchen table before going upstairs to watch another movie.

This time, Jackie gives us the love seat, but Jon's legs are so long we can't fit. He and I grab some pillows and stretch out beside each other on the carpeted floor. When I lean back into his chest, he snuggles closer and wraps an arm around my middle and a leg around one of mine. Before I can move my hair out of his face, he takes a deep breath and whispers, "Your hair smells like…strawberries."

"Yes, it's Jackie's shampoo. Like it?" I whisper back.

"Yes. Very much," he says close to my ear, with a voice that makes me shiver and gives my arms goosebumps. He rubs them away and asks if I'm cold, but I tell him that he's the reason.

"Oh," he says and runs his long fingers up and down my arm from shoulder to fingertips. On the fourth pass, I grab and hold his hand, because I don't know how much more of that I can take. Without the distraction, I focus on the movie until I hear Jon say, "Hey, sleepyhead, you're missing the best part."

Jackie rewinds what I missed, but then she decides to make popcorn and says she'll make a second batch for us. As soon as she leaves, I shift onto my back and Jon props up on an elbow to look down at me.

"I like that you fell asleep in my arms," he says.

"I was so comfy, I didn't even realize."

"Yeah, but then you started snoring."

"What? I don't snore! Do I?"

"No, you don't snore," he laughs and taps the tip of my nose with a finger that I fail to bite as he pulls away.

He looks over my face, and I think he's going to kiss me, but instead he lightly traces my brow, nose, cheeks, and jaw with his fingertips. "I love your freckles," he says. "You even have tiny ones on your ears."

"I do?"

"Yes, right here." He skims the top of my left one.

"Jonathan, are you trying to seduce me with all the touching?"

"No. You have such soft, smooth skin. I can't help but want to touch you, if that's okay."

"Just keep your touching to what's visible, please."

"Yes, ma'am," he says with a smile and places a hand on my cheek. "You're so beautiful."

I look away from those blue eyes that adore me so and turn away from his hand. "Do you mean that?" I ask.

"Of course I mean that." He turns my face back to his. "Why would you even ask such a thing?"

"I don't know…'cause I'm not," I confess, even though he's told me otherwise many times.

"What? You seriously think that?"

"My mother always tells me I'm not."

"Well, we've established she's crazy, so don't you for one second believe her. I thought so the first time I saw you. Why do you think I followed you and Marcus outside, even after you picked him over me? I wasn't interested in your friends."

"Really?"

"Yes, really," he says, with a hand traveling down my arm. "And then you were standing there after I rescued you, and you were so pissed off. You're even more beautiful when you're angry."

"I only picked him because I thought you were trouble."

"That's because I am," he says with a kiss and attacks my sides and ribs until I run out of breath.

⋏

On the third evening, Jon brings pizza and Dr. Pepper. We eat and watch another movie. This time, my back is against the love seat, and Jon's head is in my lap. Not thinking much of it, I run a hand through his short locks and flip the strands back and forth between two fingers. I don't know anyone with such bright yellow hair, much less get to play with it. I look down at my hand, and I'm amazed at how the light shines on it—like holding rays of the sun.

When Jackie gets up to go to the bathroom, Jon doesn't move. For a second, I think he's asleep, until I notice his quick, short breaths. Before I can say anything, he says, "I need you to stop playing with my hair. You've been driving me crazy for the past twenty minutes."

"Oh, I'm sorry. I didn't realize," I say as he sits up.

I'm pulled into his lap. His kisses are different this time. Not teasing with an invitation to play. Coaxing to give him more. Hungry and intensifying when I respond in kind. We don't hear Jackie come back until she says, "I'll just be downstairs getting a refill on drinks."

When she returns, the two of them go out to the side porch for a smoke. They take a while, so I do silly walks up and down the hallway until I'm overcome with curiosity and sneak over to see what's going on. The door is open, and the glass storm door is closed. They are out in the yard, near the bottom of the stairs. I listen in on their conversation.

"...and she's funny, yet serious, direct. Not silly like most girls I've known. She's more mature and knows what she wants. I've never met anyone like her," Jon says.

"She's had a hard life and had to grow up fast," Jackie tells him.

"I've gathered that from what she's told me about her parents."

"She loves you, you know?"

"Yes, I do."

"And do you feel the same?"

"Yes. I couldn't help it, no matter how much I tried not to. She's young and has her whole life ahead of her."

"Well, whatever happens with the two of you, just treat her right. She deserves it."

After a long moment, he says, "I'll do my best."

They quietly finish their cigarettes, so I sit in the chair by the door and think about the phone conversation when I finally told him I loved him.

⊥

We are about to hang up, and I respond back to his "I love you" with one of my own.

"You just said you loved me," he says.

"I did?"

"Yes, but you didn't mean to. I told you that you didn't have to say it back to me."

"Well, I said it, so I must mean it. You're the first guy I've ever said it to."

"Say it again."

"I love you," I say, to test the feel of the words and know them to be true.

"Why? Why do you love me?" he asks, using my question from our first conversation after his confession.

"Jon, I love you for the same reasons you love me."

"That's all I needed to know," he says, and I can hear him smile.

⋏

Jackie loudly fiddles with the storm door and says, "Tina's probably wondering what the hell's taking us so long."

I jump up and practically teleport twenty feet to the beginning of the hallway, where I turn around and casually walk back to the door. When they enter, I ask, "What the hell took y'all so long?"

Jackie answers as Jon takes my hand. "We were just talking for a bit."

On our way back to the living room, Jon gives me a funny look and asks, "Why are you breathing so heavy?"

I try not to look guilty and answer, "I was jogging up and down the hallway, waiting. I got bored."

We return to our positions and resume the movie, but I can't concentrate with their conversation looping in my head. I absentmindedly scratch Jon's back for about five minutes before he sits up and takes my hand. "That's not going work either," he tells me.

"Oh, sorry," I say and my hands try to find a safe place to hide. His eyes stare at me with an emotion I can't name. I finally say, "Then let's switch places, and you can scratch my back."

I move the pillow from my lap into his and place my head on it. His fingers scratch up and down my back. I can see why it bothered him, and I keep my mouth clamped shut.

When the movie ends, he still has about half an hour or so left before his ride will show up. Jackie suggests that Jon and I go for another walk or hang out in a secluded spot in the front yard. She gives me a wink as we walk out the door.

CHAPTER 15

DESIRE

Jackie's little cottage is centered on three acres. With the exception of a backyard light behind the detached garage, the surrounding forest is dark and mysterious. A rocky driveway winds along one side of the property for about two hundred feet to the street. Since we have already walked the driveway the previous evenings, Jon and I decide to check out the secluded spot.

We follow the only path, and sure enough, there's some patio furniture in a small open space. Our eyes adjust to the darkness, and I can still see his smiling face in the glow of the backyard light. We kiss until we decide to share a chair, and I make myself at home in his lap.

After placing tender kisses all over my face, he takes my hands, kisses my palms and fingertips and says, "These hands have been driving me crazy all night." I giggle and kiss him, but he breaks the kiss and whispers in my ear, "I just need to touch you."

His fingers graze my skin as they travel up my arms, across my shoulders and collarbones, and onto my neck. When his hands move into my hair, his lips surround my earlobe. Teeth and gentle sucking force my nails into his shoulder blades.

"You make such delicious noises," he says, and I realize that little moans escape with each teasing nip downward. "I want to touch you more," he pleads into my neck.

"Yes," I breathe and feel one of his hands move to my chest. Now we both make noise.

He suddenly stops and tells me to stand up. We get to our feet, and he picks me up. My legs wrap around his waist, and I receive hungry kisses in return. He lifts me higher. I cradle his head against my chest and forget all about my surprise at his strength.

We eventually reoccupy our chair, and I straddle him this time. Our mouths find each other's, and my hands play around his shoulders, onto the back of his neck, and through his hair. My skin turns goose-bumpy cold and then sugary hot as his hands meander down my spine, to my sides, and under the bottom of my shirt.

Strong fingers scratch and knead the skin of my back as the neglected side of my neck receives attention. With bracing hands, he leans me backward and presses his face to my chest. On his way back up to my ear, he gradually says, "I want to touch more of you. Can I? Please?"

As soon as I answer yes, his fingers unclasp my bra, and he takes it and my shirt off in one pull over my head. His hands return to my hair to cradle my head. After a slow, deliberate kiss, he pulls back to look in my eyes, and I realize that his hands wait patiently at my elbows.

I bite my lower lip and watch his gaze move down and linger on my nakedness. When his eyes return to mine, I finally understand desire. Over the sound of my drumming heart, he says, "Tina, you are so beautiful."

Ever so slowly, his hand moves, but his eyes remain on my face when he grips me gently. I suck in a breath and see him smile. My eyes close, and my head drops back. A new sensation grips me. I tingle and ache. He leans me backward, once again, but this time his mouth and free hand work together. I moan his name.

The surrounding forest listens to us until the roar of a vehicle down the distant road passes the house and ends our attempts to know each other more. His mouth returns to mine for a final kiss before he helps me get dressed.

I walk him to the road, where we hold each other as the headlights make their way back to us. He twice offers to escort me back to the house, but I tell him, "No, that's okay. I need a moment to collect myself before going back in."

He laughs and says, "I could use a long walk myself. I'll call you tomorrow. I love you."

"I love you. Sweet dreams."

He replies with a smirk, "You too."

A pickup truck pulls into the driveway, and Nick sticks his head out the window with a happy hello.

⁂

After the departure of that noisy truck, my mind fills with those intimate moments. I take my dear, sweet time and barely hear the crunching rocks beneath my feet. I notice the lingering smell of Jon's cologne and think I'll never get used to him saying that he loves me.

When I reach the house, I open the door and instantly turn red. Jackie waits at the kitchen table with an expectant look on her face and curiosity practically beaming out of her green cat eyes. "Well?" she asks.

"I let him get to second base," I reply.

"Nice. Need a cigarette or a drink?" she giggles as I take a seat.

"No, but he might," I say with a grin, and we both laugh. She passes me the metal bowl of leftover popcorn and says, "From the way you two were making out, I'm surprised you haven't done more."

I shake my head and explain, "We haven't had any alone time before. We're always in public places with other people. Thanks for all of this, by the way."

"That's what Aunt Jackies are for," she says with a nod.

Once we are down to the kernels, she tells me, "I think you picked well with this one."

"You really think so?"

"Yes, he's handsome, and he loves you."

"I know."

"Yes, but when we were outside earlier, I had a little talk with him, and he told me so. Hope you don't mind."

"No, it's fine. I caught the end of it anyway."

"I was hoping you were listening."

"Jackie, you are so bad," I say, shaking my head.

"So, you gonna share any details?"

"No…well…just one thing. At one point, he told me to stand up, and I'm like okay. And then he picked me up by my ass and had me up in the air to get to my chest."

"Oh, Tina! Sex with him will be fabulous."

CHAPTER 16

Confession

Summer is almost over. I have one week left until school starts, and I still live at my cousin Rachel's house. Mother continues to search for a place we can afford in my school district. Until then, Iris's gracious father has agreed to let me move in with them.

Jon calls me for our usual afternoon chat, but I remember that today is Saturday, and I will to see him tonight. As soon as he speaks, I know something isn't right.

"Are you coming to the pool hall tonight?" he asks.

"As far as I know, unless my mom flakes out."

"Just make sure you're there. I'll talk to you tonight."

"Okay? You called me just to confirm? You don't want to talk?"

"Not now. I'll talk to you then."

"Alright. See you tonight. Love you."

He hesitates before saying "I love you," but before I can say anything more, he hangs up.

The next day, I answer the phone, and he says, "Hey. What happened to you last night? I was there and waited, but you never showed up. I called, and no one answered."

"Sorry. My mom came home and didn't want to take me, so we got into a huge fight, and I couldn't call you. Now I'm forbidden to go to Jackie's house, and I can't date until I'm eighteen."

"What? Tina, I'm so sorry."

"It's not your fault."

"No. It is my fault. If it wasn't for me…dammit."

"Jon, I'm the one who mouthed off to her. It's no big deal. She wasn't serious. At least, I hope not."

"No, I'm sorry, but I have to do this now. I'm sorry for what I'm about to tell you."

"What?" I say, confused.

"I wanted to tell you last night in person."

"Jon, you're scaring me."

"I should have told you from the start. I tried to tell you a bunch of times, but you looked at me with those big brown eyes and your sweetness, and I couldn't do it."

"Jonathan, what the hell are you talking about?" I brace myself for the worst—always the worst, because I intimately know the feeling of doom.

"We're over. I have to end us. I should have never started something I knew was pointless, that had no future."

"Jonathan," I whisper as I repeat his words in my head to make sure I heard what I refuse to believe.

"Tina, I'm sorry."

"Why? Why?" I calmly question, but my head screeches. "Did I do something wrong? Is it because I'm so young?"

"No. Nothing like that."

"Then what? Another girl?"

"I, um…yes."

"Bullshit, Jon!" I shout, because I know he's lying. "You don't act the way you do with me and say the things you do and there be another girl. I don't believe that for one fucking moment, so don't even try! What's the real reason?" I demand. My mind races through every interaction and conversation and finds nothing to doubt.

"I…no. You're right, there's no other girl. There's only ever been you."

"Then what is it?" I ask and try not to hyperventilate. "What could be worse than that? You never loving me would be worse," I say, the last part more to myself.

"I talked to my father recently, and he warned me before, but I didn't listen to him."

"Explain! Goddamn it!"

"I joined the military. Before we met, I joined the army to be in the Special Forces like…"

"Like your father," I finish, and remember his parents' difficulties.

"He told me not to get involved. He told me to sow my oats or whatever if I needed to, and I did, but I couldn't do that with you or anyone else after we met."

"Why didn't you tell me at the beginning?"

"I told you that first night I wasn't interested in a relationship or a girlfriend, remember?"

"Oh, don't you even! You did this! You were warned by your own father, and I told you I didn't want a boyfriend, and still you gave me your number and…" I say, angry and hurt, but betrayal enters the fray, "You…you lied to me."

"I never lied to you."

"Other than telling me this was all because of a girl just now!"

"Tina, I know. I'm sorry. I thought it would be easier if you thought…I never lied to you about anything else."

"Easier for who? You never told me any different. Same thing as lying, Jon! You deceive me, tell me you love me, let me fall in love with you, and then this! Was it all some kind of game to you?"

"No, I'm sorry. I should have told you, but every time I tried, I couldn't do it. I thought Marcus told you that day he apologized."

"So, is that why you told me you loved me?"

"No, of course not! I told you because you asked, and it was true."

I hesitate. "Was true."

"Tina, I can't love you anymore. I have to let you go. I'm leaving in a week. I'll have a life out in the world, and I won't be back for a long time, for years. You have your life here. You'll get over me and grow up and…"

"Up until six minutes ago, my life had you in it and now nothing, and I'm supposed to get over it…get over you just like that? Why didn't you explain before? Wait a minute. A week? One week? Why did you wait until a week before you leave?"

"Tina, it doesn't matter. I'm leaving, and we are over. All I can say is that I'm sorry, and I hope one day you can forgive me."

I lose my voice as I accept that nothing will change this new reality. My thoughts become a howling scream of rage and pain, accompanied by shaking hands and fast breaths.

"Tina, say something."

"I…I hate you! The next girl you kiss, I hope you think of me, and it tortures you."

I hang up, and the phone rings immediately. I answer, thinking it's him, and I'm ready to yell every obscenity I know, but I hear Iris's voice. "Tina, it's me. I just got into a huge fight with Nick. Did Jon call you?"

"Yes," I say, still not crying, still not able to process what happened.

"And?"

I say the words, "He broke up with me," and swallow their bitterness.

"That son of a bitch!" she yells away from the phone and then continues, "Nick just told me what was happening, and we got into a huge fight, and I hung up on him and called you. I'm so sorry!"

"Iris, I don't…I don't know what happened. One minute he's professing his undying love, and now it's over."

"Did you sleep with him?"

"No."

"Good, but I bet he tried."

"No, actually, he was a gentleman, and now it doesn't even matter."

"Tina, I'm sorry. If I would have known, I never would have encouraged you at Chloe's party. That rat bastard! Both of them! Are you okay?"

"I don't know. I got into it with my mom about Jon last night. That's why I didn't show up, and I'm not allowed to date till I'm eighteen, and it was all for nothing," I say quietly.

"Tina, I think you're in shock. You're not even crying."

"Iris…I can't. If I start, I don't think I'll be able to stop."

From a distance, somewhere in the house, Mother yells, "Tina Marie, get off the phone with that boy right this minute!"

"Iris, I've got to go. I'll call you later."

"Yeah, I'm going to call Nick back and scream at him some more. I'll talk to you later."

As I hang up, Mother comes into the living room and demands, "Did you tell him you can't date until you're eighteen?"

"No, Mother, we broke up, so it doesn't even matter."

"Oh, well, you…"

"Mother, for once, please don't. Not right now," I say with watery eyes, and I go to my borrowed room.

⁂

Mother leaves me alone. Iris calls back, but I refuse to talk to her or anyone else who calls to check on me. I hear my cousin Rachel tell Iris, "She won't even eat, and she won't come out of her room. I'll have her call you when she's ready."

After the second day of me not eating, Mother forces me out of bed and pushes me into the bathroom to take a shower. When I stand there motionless, she threatens, "Either you can do it yourself, or I'll put you in, clothes and all, and turn the water on."

I comply. After I'm done, I sit in complete silence as she combs and blow-dries my hair, something she hasn't done since I was little.

Rachel won't let me do anything else until I eat something, so I chew a piece of toast, but I don't taste it. For the rest of the week, she makes me eat breakfast, lunch, and dinner.

They won't let me stay locked up in my room, so I sit on the couch all day and stare at nothing until I fall asleep. After a few days of me sleeping on the couch, Rachel hands me a big spoon and a newly opened container of mint chocolate chip ice cream. I manage all of one sentence, and she passes me a box of tissue.

⁂

On Friday, I finally talk to Iris, who tells me Jon will leave on Sunday. She tries to convince me to meet him at the pool hall one last time. He wants to say goodbye and get his belongings that I ended up with. I finally tell her I'll think about it. When I hang up, I begin a whole new round of crying.

Mother immediately makes a phone call. An hour later, Jackie picks me up, which is a good idea until we enter her house. I see Jon everywhere I look.

Jackie suggests we make a bonfire and burn his stuff out in the front yard. I place each item onto the woodpile, and she hands me some lighter fluid. I look at the bottle, pop off the cap, and change my mind. She gives me a ride and waits in the parking lot.

Before I exit the car, she says, "Tina, you don't owe him anything. Toss his crap in the garbage, and tell him to go to hell."

"I know, Jackie, I should, but I want to say goodbye."

"Yeah, say goodbye, and slap him for good measure."

I stare at the entrance and see us standing there, him with a confession, and me on his lips. I think about the wasted hope and the possibilities of a life with someone who actually loves me. I enter the building, determined to throw the things in my hands at him and then slap him in the face.

Iris waits for me at the row of glass double doors and tells me that Jon wants me to come in. I refuse. "Does he want a scene in front of everyone? Tell him he can get his sorry ass out here and get his crap himself."

"That's what I told him you would say," she says and closes the door.

While I wait, I pace back and forth across the hallway and gather an arsenal of words to shout at him. I halt at the sound of the closing door and realize he's standing near me. When I look at his face, my determination and anger falter. I say nothing as I hand him what is rightfully his.

A traitorous tear escapes. He wipes it away and says, "Tina, you'll be okay. It will take time, but you'll have guys falling all over themselves soon enough, and you'll forget all about me."

"Is that why you imagined another guy kissing me that day?"

He hesitates and then quietly answers, "It doesn't matter now."

"None of it matters now," I whisper and look away. Even though I know my face tells him plenty, I keep my shit together and refuse to let him see me really cry. Neither of us say anything more, so I turn around, and within five steps, he calls after me, "Tina, wait."

I freeze at his request, and when I don't turn around, I hear him put his belongings on the ground. He enters my line of vision, but I continue to stare at the tile floor until his hand lifts my chin. He says, "I don't have the right to ask, but can I kiss you one last time?"

"Why, Jonathan?" I answer, to which he replies, "Do you really have to ask?"

I can't respond, because he kisses me anyway. I don't step back, and I don't stop him. My mouth betrays me and ignores the screaming in my head. When his arms go around me, my arms go around him, but I refuse to feel his kiss.

He doesn't understand how lost I was until he found me. What it took for me to let down my walls, to trust him, to tell him what little he knows about my parents, to accept him as a part of my life believing he would be a constant, fixed point, a steady light in the dark chaos. Normal never wins.

When we let go of each other, I feel his fingers run through the ends of my hair. I step back, and he puts a hand to my face, but I flinch and move out of his reach. "Don't touch me like that!" I snap with hate. "Don't ever touch me again!"

His hand drops, and he doesn't move. I dare not look back at his face and glance around to find something else to focus on. Iris remains at the doors. Her sympathetic face keeps me steady as I listen to the sound of Jon collecting his things from the floor. He turns and walks to the door, but Iris glares at him and refuses to move out of the way. He opens the door to her left and goes in without looking back.

I turn around and quickly walk toward the building exit. When Iris calls my name, I run.

CHAPTER 17

MISERY

Before Mother drops me and my suitcase off at Iris's house, we go to a beauty salon. I want to be rid of the constant reminder of Jon that follows me around. Everyone at school is surprised, because long hair is the norm. I get many compliments, and a few guys I don't know say that I look pretty and remind them of a dark-haired Molly Ringwald.

Life as a sophomore eventually becomes bearable as the hours fill with projects, homework, and weekends with my best friends, but I harbor misery as I watch them with their boyfriends. I decide to visit Mother on the weekends to avoid being a third wheel.

⁂

On a Friday, during after-lunch free time, Iris finds me out on the steps by the school parking lot and tells me someone wants to talk to me. I go into the atrium to find Scott, in his football jersey, standing alone near the doors. Still as handsome and sweet as ever, he asks me out on a date. *Fat chance of that happening now.*

"As much as I would like to, Scott, I can't."

"And why not?" he asks, with a fold of arms across his chest and a playful look of disappointment.

Unprepared for the question, I think of my mother, my current homelessness, Jonathan, and the dating restrictions now in full force. I pick the one that hurts the most and say, "Honestly, I met a guy over the summer who broke my heart, and I'm not over him yet." *And how the hell did that just happen? He asks, and I just answer. Open and honest. I barely know him.*

"Oh," he says, surprised, and then looks at me with concern. "Tina, the jerk didn't deserve you."

"True," I say and try not to frown. I glace away as my brain focuses on the past and not the present. When I realize I've been quiet for too long, I look back up to see his golden brown, not blue eyes watching me. For a split second, I imagine a future in which he walks me to class again. "That's very sweet of you to say," I tell him with a half smile.

He replies, "Well, when you're ready, I'll be waiting."

Now I'm the one with the surprised face. "Oh, I, uh, yeah," I stammer out before pulling myself together. "You'll be the first to know."

"I'll hold you to that," he promises with a grin. "See you around."

"See you later, Scott," I say with a grin of my own, and he responds as he walks away, "I hope sooner than later."

I laugh, shaking my head at our banter, and feel less like a ghost until he disappears into the bustling crowd of our fellow students.

Iris practically runs me over when I open the door to return to my spot on the steps.

"So, what happened?" she asks.

"Nothing," I say and see the hope drain away.

"What? Tina! That's the third one you've run off. It's been almost three months. You have to get over him."

I tell her that there's no one I want, I never want to fall in love again, and I never want to get married. When she tells me that I might meet someone after high school, I say, "Iris, at that point, I'll just fuck whoever I want and not ever worry about being tied down."

From the look on her face, she's shocked, but I don't care.

CHAPTER 18

DRUGS

In a moment of desperation or most likely straight-up stupidity, Mother moves into a house between two of her ex-boyfriends, one being the ever-popular mustached Jim. Right after Christmas break, I'm forced to move there as well, and I origami myself back into a life with Mother. Once again, I say goodbye and start over at a new school. I go through the motions of being the newbie and return to quiet loner status.

Everything is peachy keen for about a month until Jim becomes an active participant in Mother's business, again, and all goes to hell in a handbasket. The house always reeks of pot, and Mother begins to disappear. Then, several times a week, I come home from school to find the house completely trashed. Apparently, Mother and Jim are often home during the day.

On one such idiotic afternoon, I leave the house as is. Mother and Jim arrive in the evening, and she begins to caterwaul because the house is still trashed. I mention the dinner they neglected to bring home, and they leave to get it.

I half-ass clean their mess and settle back down to play Nintendo with Eric. Two hours later, they return with pizza. Eric and I already ate sandwiches, so we keep playing.

After about ten minutes, I can't help but notice Mother and Jim's argument and frantic search. They ask me what happened to the bag full of pot, and I tell them that I don't keep up with their drugs.

"You cleaned the house! Where the fuck did you put it?" Mother yells at me.

"I didn't put it anywhere!" I shout back, not taking my eyes off the screen, because hell if Eric is going to win again. I hear Jim open the garbage can, but I already know it's empty because I took the trash out to the street for pickup in the morning.

Mother threatens to beat me with a belt and hits me all of one time across my right arm and back before I'm out there at nine o'clock at night digging through the garbage like a homeless person. Toward the bottom of the second bag, I find a rolled-up gallon baggie of mostly seeds.

⋏

The next week, I come home from school and lose my shit.

Mother, Jim, and a couple of strangers are on my bed with a mirror. I witness a line of white powder disappear and shout, "I'm calling the cops!"

Mother can't do anything but beg me not to call. Infuriated, I watch the entire one minute it takes for Jim and the strangers to pack up and leave. I slam and lock the door behind them and then open Mother's bedroom door. *I hate my life.* She's passed out facedown on top of her bed.

I grab a handful of change from her purse. With a black garbage bag and my backpack slung over my shoulders, I walk down the road to the washateria. I do my homework while I wait for my blanket and sheets. Dinner is a vending machine Payday candy bar and a Dr. Pepper. Two hours later, I roll my eyes when I find Mother still passed out in the same position.

A month or so later, big shocker, we move again, but this time the house is only a few blocks away on Magnolia Street.

CHAPTER 19
UNICORNS

When I was a young child, I loved unicorns. They were magical and beautiful and pure of heart. I had a menagerie of items—posters, paintings, snow globes, bells, and knickknacks of various sizes.

My favorites among them were the five-inch-tall, white porcelain figurines with shiny golden hooves and single, spiraling, golden horns. I never played with them, for they were sacred to me. I would clean them and arrange them for display. When all the moving began, I would lovingly wrap them in newspapers and pack them carefully together each time.

We never stayed in one place long. One by one, the collection dwindled, breaking one right after the other like pieces of me as time went by. After a few years, I stopped unpacking them and hid the box in closet after closet.

A teenager now, I'm too old to believe in unicorns; nonetheless, I unfold the newspapers with care and examine the six figurines and the one large snow globe that has survived with me.

I place them on the built-in shelf above my desk, which is across from my closet, all of which are under my loft bed.

I adore the Magnolia Street house. It's nothing fancy, but it has a wide front porch with a white bench swing and a large yard that surrounds us. I particularly love the singing rain when it meets the metal roof. Most importantly, I love my pretty room. The walls are teal and purple. I can climb my bed's side ladder, lay on the mattress, and look out the windows that line one side of my bed and go almost to the floor. The little panes of glass, dozens of perfect small squares all in rows, are covered by teal and purple curtains.

The rest of my room is an empty void. I don't have additional furniture yet, which is okay. I learned quickly as an eight-year-old that something is better than nothing.

When Mother took us and fled to Dallas prior to the divorce, my siblings and I shared one pillow and a blanket on a carpeted apartment bedroom floor. I cried as we huddled on the floor together while Mother slept in her room on the one mattress we owned.

After the divorce, the judge allowed us to return to our family home to pack our belongings. Like the last time, we fit what we could in the car. Upon Mother's solo third trip to retrieve more, she found the house empty. Apparently, my father got rid of everything before he disappeared to Chicago. What he couldn't sell or give away met a fiery fate in our backyard. Mother allowed us to see the house for ourselves. I sifted through the ashes of the burn pile with my foot and found the charred remains of Eric's train set.

So here I am, seven years later, with a built-in loft bed in a bedroom I can call my own. No more sharing space with Jenny. Mother promises this move will be our last, but plans constantly change. I've attended three high schools, two junior highs, and about six elementary schools between fourth and fifth grade. After the fifteenth time I had to repack my belongings, I quit counting homes. She's putting an unprecedented amount of effort into fixing up and decorating this one, so I have hope that her promise may come true.

CHAPTER 20

MAIL

Out the front door I go, down the porch steps, and across the short sidewalk to the street where our black mailbox stands at attention. I open the metal door and see a week's worth of papers stuffed tight. I fish out our first stack of mail.

On my way back to the house, I rummage through it all and find a white envelope addressed to me. I think Iris has written me again, but then I notice the military insignias. The rest of the mail drops on the porch as I sit on the steps. With eyes glued to the letter in my hands, I debate whether to burn it whole or in pieces like tiny white birthday candles. I open it instead.

Jon's neat cursive writing tells me that since he left, he's thought of me every day. My words came true when he kissed another girl. All he could think of was my eyes, my lips, my dimpled cheeks, and his hands in my hair. He never stopped loving me and wants me to know how he really feels, even though I hate him now. With deep regret, he asks for forgiveness and requests that I write back. The letter ends with "Love always, Jonathan."

He left me. He left me like Father left an empty house and a pit of ashes. If he would have just told me the whole truth, I could have let him go. Not hollowed out and ripped apart. Can't and won't do that shit again. I hate him. I don't need him. I don't need anyone. What I need is a lighter.

No. I hate what he did to me. I was forced to let go, to hate him so I could exist on my own. A return to darkness after playing in the sunshine. Memories that burn. Memories of a normal life beyond Mother. No fear. Safe. A life of my own with laughter and kindness. I was beautiful and cherished. Loved. Loved.

After weeks of deliberation, I write back. More letters are exchanged, which leads to random long-distance phone calls and surprise appearances on my doorstep whenever he can come home.

CHAPTER 21

BROKEN

Right outside my bedroom door, Mother entertains her friends in the smoky living room which reeks of pot. The blaring radio is often drowned out by their conversation and laughter.

Meanwhile, my little bro and I are bored out of our minds, and since there is still a wide-open space in my room, the roughhousing begins. We make a ton of racket as we run at the wall, kick a foot up, and push ourselves to see how far we can jump back.

After Mother yells at us to stop literally bouncing off the walls, we decide to play Superman, a silly game we've played since we were small. I'm always the flying machine because Eric's toothpick-legged, skinny ass can't hold me up.

I lay on the floor on my back with my feet together, straight up in the air. He lies straight and still as possible with his chest on my feet. He teeters for a moment until we find the perfect balance. Not too far left or right. We count how long he can stay without falling over. Sometimes I make him fall over on purpose. When that gets old, we try one foot.

Bored with simplicity, we play cannonball. I pick him up the same as Superman, but only partially so I can push him backward. My goal is to see how far I can toss him, and his goal is to land on his feet. We get pretty good and decide to up the ante by pushing him farther and farther each time.

"Push me super hard this time, and let's see how far I can go," Eric says, with a gleam in his eyes.

"Are you sure you can land?" I ask. He's pretty light, and I have strong legs.

"I've got this!" he reassures me.

I move back, closer to the far wall, and at seventy-five percent power, I send him flying through the air. He lands, not on his feet but close to under my bed. We freeze and wait for Mother to yell, but when nothing happens, we burst out laughing. As he gets up, I say, "You should have seen your face when you fell."

He says, "That was awesome! Let's try it again!"

Mother yells, "Tina! Eric!"

"Sorry, Mom!" I yell back and try not to laugh as I play back in my mind Eric's flailing arms and legs.

He lands perfectly on his feet on the second try, and we high five.

"I can launch you farther," I tell him.

"Really?" he asks, and I nod my head. "Oh, hell yeah. Let's do this!"

He gets back into position. I push with all my might, and he rockets backward. Eric's bottom half sticks the landing, but his top half crashes into the window. I jump up and run to him, praying to God nothing is broken—meaning the window.

He's fine, but he's frozen in place. I hold his arms until he can stand straight.

Luckily, the curtain helped prevent any damage. I straighten it as I listen and watch my bedroom door. My heart stops with the tinkle of glass on the wood floor. Beneath the curtain, I find two small, rectangular pieces of glass that would otherwise fit perfectly together.

I pull back the curtain. To make sure I'm not imagining things, I put my hand through the single gaping square of darkness and feel cool air. The other panels in the section and everything else is intact. *Oh, thank you God! This could have been so much worse. My punishment will be bad, but at least The Queen of Hearts will let me keep my head.*

I send a pleading prayer to God for mercy from Mother's wrath, but no miracles for me today. I spin around to face her when my door flies open.

"What the fuck happened?" she says with venom through clenched teeth.

"It's nothing. No big deal. Eric and I were horseplaying, and I pushed him too far. Everything is fine," I say in denial and push the pieces of glass back under the curtain with the heel of my foot. *Please don't check the window!*

She stalks toward me with death in her eyes.

"Mom, it's nothing major. It can be fixed," I say.

She pushes me aside and pulls the curtain back. It takes her a moment to see the damage.

"You fat, lying bitch! You call this nothing?" she screams at me.

"Mom, I'm sorry! It was an accident! It's only a small piece. Please don't be mad. It was an accident," I plead.

"You want to break things? I'll show you breaking things!" she yells and looks around my room. With one hand, she grabs three unicorn figurines off my shelf and throws them like a baseball pitcher to the wall across my room.

"*Nooo!*" I scream and watch them explode into a million white pieces. The shards fall and scatter all over the floor. A white indention mars the light purple paint. She grabs two more. I run to the wall to block her from throwing them and barely feel the broken pieces crunch under my socks. "Please! They're all I have left!" I beg, but they almost hit me, and pieces fly into my hair.

I know nothing will appease her. Once she's angry, there's no stopping her. I have no choice but to wait until she runs out of steam.

"Get out of the way, Tina Marie!" she shouts.

"No, please don't throw anymore! I'm sorry! I've learned my lesson. Please!" I cry.

"No? Was that a no?" she growls, but I don't answer because nothing I say will matter. She throws the last unicorn down on the floor in front of her and stomps on it. I run and slide to the floor, hoping it isn't broken. I scoop it up.

"So, you want to say no to me," she says, laughing, and proceeds to violently ransack my room. I back up to the door and stay out of her way, because for once, I'm not the one suffering at her hands.

She swipes my belongings off my desk, rips the curtains down, and kicks it all to the far wall. She opens my closet. All my folded and hanging clothes and shoes join the pile of school books, notebooks, pens, pencils, my backpack, jacket, and the former figurines. The contents of unpacked boxes join the heap. I have nothing left for her to destroy save my bed above her head, but I'm wrong again.

I rush at her as she grabs the snow globe. Glass shatters behind me. Facing the window, I sink to my knees and stare at the reflected room and that dark and empty missing piece. My eyes move to her reflection when she threatens, "Now clean it up, or I'll throw it all outside!" She slams the door behind her, and the wall quakes in response.

I continue to kneel and stare at the black missing square until I can no longer feel my legs. The top of my jeans is wet from all the useless tears running down my face.

When I finally sit back to stretch my numb legs, I notice tiny spots of blood on the bottom of my white socks. I brace myself for the pain of removing them and stop because I still have the last unicorn in my hand. I open my fingers. Her two back legs sit in my palm, separated from her body, and her horn is missing. "I know exactly how you feel," I whisper to her.

Once my pain-filled legs are fully back to life, I peel my socks off, and the shards come out with them. The cuts aren't deep. I hobble to the bathroom, wash my face and my feet, and apply a few tiny bandages.

After getting the broom, dust pan, a garbage bag, and some towels, I return to my room to begin the process of disaster recovery. I know the drill. She likes to destroy our rooms if they aren't cleaned to her specifications, but today is special. I have sharps bits and glittery wet things to contend with, so I dig out a matching pair of dry shoes to protect my feet. *High heels will have to do.*

I find what is left of the snow globe. One sharp, jagged piece of glass arcs up over the off-kilter unicorn. *Oh, how the glitter used to swirl and shimmer, contained in spherical form.* I take the music box out of the broken bottom and turn the knob to see if it still functions. "Somewhere Over the Rainbow" makes me sob. When the cylinder stops rotating, and the tiny tines become silent, I place the little metal contraption on my shelf, next to the legs and body of the former unicorn.

I slowly and carefully separate everything into piles. I wipe up what I can of the water and glitter from the wall and floor as I go. I sweep up the glass and porcelain bits as I find them. The wet clothes and curtains go in my laundry hamper to be washed tomorrow. I find a pair of clean pajamas under my overturned desk chair. The dry clothes go back into the closet, and I repack one of the moving boxes.

I return all the school supplies to their home on the desk, except for a few textbooks and a notebook. Within fifteen minutes, my arms tire from holding the blow-dryer, and I close the wrinkled, damp pages. With my scissors, I fashion a temporary covering out of a divider page from a three-subject notebook. After I tape the manila square over the gap in the window, I look past my reflection into the dark beyond and wonder if anyone out there witnessed what occurred. All other thoughts become obscure, and I continue to stare out the window like a solemn, wingless statue in a cemetery. My head is a whirlwind as I analyze what went wrong and devise scenarios for what I could have done or will do next time. I berate myself for not doing something more to stop her.

The nonstop replay abruptly ends when my door creaks open and Mother says, "Make sure this is spotless before I get home tomorrow."

I turn to survey the huge mess I have left and politely say, "Yes, ma'am."

When she shuts the door, I climb up the loft ladder to check my alarm clock. It's almost eleven thirty. *School should be fun tomorrow. Homework or dinner?* I grab a piece of cold pepperoni pizza out of the Little Caesars box and swallow it before I clean the kitchen.

Since the whole neighborhood now has a view of my room, I change clothes in the bathroom.

Oh, look. There's that wraith again. Nice to see you. Been a few months. You look the same, but your face isn't blemished this time. Ah, but the eyes, so hollow. Should we discuss suicide? No, not yet? Alright then. See ya soon.

Finally in bed, I stare blankly into the nothingness of my dark room. *A promise is a promise. I won't let her win. I will be better than her. I will have a better life.*

I open my soul to heaven and wonder if anyone ever hears my pain and sorrows. I never ask for Mother to change or for bad things to befall her. I pray for strength to endure and the wisdom to do what's right. I pray until I fall asleep.

CHAPTER 22
WISHES

Spring of 1994 arrives, and I sit in another wooden chair, talking to another judge. No, Mother was not arrested again. She did something right, thanks to Eric. Last fall, during a peaceful morning with the four of us piled in Mother's bed, Eric explained a comic book he was reading. Inspired, Mother formed a brilliant plan to solve our family's second biggest problem. Our middle-class life was flushed down the toilet with the divorce.

⁂

Life in poverty is a predictable game of cat and mouse. We live where we can afford, and move when the rent isn't paid. I particularly remember the rundown trailer park where a stabbed man walked up with blood gushing from his gut and casually asked to borrow the phone. If the car payments are nonexistent, Mother misses work, and we won't move far. God forbid anyone becomes sick or seriously injured. We'll have even less money when Mother misses work to sit up at the Huey P. Long Medical Center emergency room for six hours. Come to think of it, we go to the doctor, dentist, and eye doctor only when absolutely necessary.

The house phone is an ordinary object until I pick it up and realize I'm holding a carcass against my face. I ignore its useless body until Mother gives me another new number to memorize. Periodically, I come home to find the utilities shut off too, which leads to food in ice chests and no air conditioning. I never fail to stare at the ceiling light and flip the wall switch like it's going to magically work if I flip faster.

We don't have central air anyway. The one window air-conditioning unit in the living room does a piss-poor job of cooling the whole house. Ceiling and box fans are our best friends. Sticky summer nights are the worst. Drenched in sweat, I flip over to give my front some relief with a hot breeze as opposed to hot, damp sheets. The rotisserie game continues until one of us gives up first, and we all pile into the living room to sleep.

Winters are better. In each room, we have these old, metal, rectangular gas heaters that look like miniature radios from back in the 1950s. We light them with one of Mother's cigarette lighters or a burning piece of rolled-up newspaper lit by the kitchen stove. Right before the flame reaches the hiss of the gas, I screw my eyes shut and hold my breath, as if doing so will prevent me from going out in a blaze of glory. When I wake up to particularly cold days, I shut the doors in the kitchen and turn on the stove and oven. The burning gas quickly makes the small kitchen nice and cozy so we can take turns getting dressed.

The colorful food stamp money for our once-a-month grocery shopping trips sometimes doesn't last to the next month.

Correction. *My* once-a-month trip. Mother drops me off at the store. The buggy is always overflowing with the cheapest food I can find. I want to die of embarrassment when I'm at the checkout line, ripping out the money from the booklet. I always look around and hope I don't run into someone from school. Afterward, I have the pleasure of waiting outside for Mother to show back up.

We don't own a dishwasher or microwave, but since we moved to the Magnolia Street house, we finally have a washing machine and dryer. They sit on the screened-in back porch with the fridge. Thankfully, no more Sundays are spent at the washateria, but yeah, they're tricky. We must manually turn the water on and off at the wall spicket for each cycle. I sometimes forget and wade through a river flowing across the back porch, which isn't the worst part. When we first moved in, wet, bare feet or shoes in combination with the metal spicket meant electrocution. The first time I met the requirements, my brain took a moment to register the new sensation. Numb. Tingling. Trembling. *Pain*! I jumped back with a yelp of, "Son of a bitch!" and splashed water up my jeans. In the river, I held my forearm and flexed my otherwise normal hand. I warned Mother and my siblings, but nothing was done. After a few jolts each, my siblings and I learned to jump over the river and onto a wooden chair next to the washer. I got smart, and we now use a pair of yellow rubber gloves.

If something in the house truly breaks, a family friend either fixes the problem, we figure out how to rig a solution, or we wait ages until Mother can save up enough money. One time, a water pipe broke out in the yard, and I spent nearly three weeks turning the water on and off at the street so we could take showers and flush toilets.

⋏

Mother put her plan into action and scrounged up enough funds to hire a bounty hunter. Father was promptly escorted from Chicago to Louisiana. It was high time he faced the music. He owed upward of a hundred thousand dollars in back child support. He never paid a cent after the second court order of nine hundred dollars a month, an increase from three hundred. Apparently, we were only worth a hundred each when they got divorced, which he paid only three times.

Once my father was in custody, a third judge slapped him with a jail sentence. We visited him twice—the only contact in eight years. I didn't say much as I peered through the bars at him. All I could think about was how we gave up calling when everyone refused speak to us; the birthdays and Christmases gone by without a word; and to top it off, his new family.

⋏

Father's incarceration is cut short for good behavior, which leads me to this fourth judge with the kind face who asks, "Is there anything you want? If you could have anything, what would it be?"

"Anything?" I ask, but I already know my answer.

"Anything," he replies with a smile.

"Braces!" I say and cover my mouth because I practically shouted into the microphone.

"Why do you want braces, young lady?"

I smile my biggest smile possible, which is the one thing I avoid doing.

"I see," he says before asking, "Anything else?"

I glance at Mother on the right and see her new husband, Vinny, smiling at me from behind her. I focus for a moment on my father, who is on the left. I turn to the judge with my request, "I would like to visit my father and his side of the family in Chicago."

I hear Mother suck in a breath. *There's going to be hellfire and brimstone when I get home.*

"And why do you want to do that?" the judge asks.

"Because I haven't seen any of my family in almost ten years, and I miss them. My grandparents, my aunt and uncle. I want to get to know them again."

I feel the menace radiating off Mother, but I don't look at her.

"Very well," the judge says.

My father agrees to the terms of his release—back to jail if he misses one payment, garnished income tax checks until the full amount of back child support is paid off, and the requirement to pay for his children's requests.

Yes, we get our wishes, but I will pay too.

Eric, Jenny, and I wait with Vinny in a hallway. Mother signs the final paperwork behind closed doors. Vinny looks at me, shakes his head, and gives me a quick hug. "You've got big cojones, kid," he says to me. "Dragon Lady will be on a rampage when we get home, but it will be worth it. Just try to get through tonight."

"Thanks. I know. I always do," I say to the old man. I look at his wrinkly, tan face and feel sorry for him. *He didn't know what he was getting into. We all tried to tell him. He'll be gone soon.*

⋏

Armageddon starts the moment Mother enters the house. I run to my room to lock the door, but I'm too slow. She slaps me as usual, grabs my hair, and slings me onto the couch in my room. Vinny intercedes and threatens to beat her ass with his walking cane if she touches me again.

He sits beside me on the couch as Godzilla rampages through the house, throwing things and screaming about how I betrayed her and betrayed our family, and how could I do such a thing, and how I don't love my own mother, and blah, blah, blah, blah.

An explanation is pointless, so I tune her out, pull my legs up, and hug my knees. My face hides in my arms to keep her from seeing the glee I have planted on it. *I get my wishes and there's nothing you can do about it. Ha!*

The contents of my desk hit the floor, so I jump up and yell with a finger in her face, "You're lucky I didn't tell that judge all about you!"

She drops my stuff, stomps out of my room, and slams her bedroom door. Vinny and I sit in silence for a minute or two before we look at each other. I give him a grin. The shock on his face from my mother's behavior turns to understanding. He gets up to leave, but before he shuts the door, he says with a small smile, "Like I said, kid, big cojones."

CHAPTER 23
REFUGE

A year zooms by, and as of March of my junior year, I'm happily settled into my new school. Within the confines of that building, I laugh, dream, and hope. I have a sense of purpose, the companionship of friends, a consistent schedule, and a meal I don't have to cook and serve. Adults are kind and praise my efforts. I smile more, my teeth currently sporting silver wires and green and blue bands for spring. Guys show interest, but I decline all invitations.

My best friend, Andrew, is a shiny star in my otherwise bleak and weary life. He is like a big brother to me. Technically, I'm the big sister by five months, but he wins by a foot and a half in height. At the beginning of the school year, I stayed quietly in my shell, but out of nowhere, Andrew appeared and wouldn't stop talking to me. At first, I was leery, but after we both agreed romance was not on the table, I discovered we have a lot in common, and he has a knack for making me laugh. Now, we save seats for each other before our classes, and I never have to eat lunch alone.

He's the only person at school I trust, but I keep him away from Mother as much as possible. True to form, she often embarrasses me in public and in front of friends. If she's feeling extra diabolical, everyone enjoys a "Dairy Queen" temper tantrum. My siblings and I sat low in the booth the day she turned into a harpy and threw her pickled cheeseburger at the unsuspecting girls behind the counter.

Andrew knows something with Mother is off, but I won't talk about it, so he keeps me busy and preoccupied with better things. Against my protests, he dragged me to meetings for all of his different school clubs and activities. We now both actively participate, and I find more to school than lessons, homework, and twirling a flag for the color guard.

We often hang out at his house and play video games until the wee hours of Saturday and Sunday. Recently, my morning routine includes a walk to his house before school. I bang on his bedroom window and remind him that senior skip days don't apply to us yet. During those mornings, I eat breakfast at the kitchen table and watch cable TV, both of which I don't have at home.

In the afternoons, before the final school bell rings, I watch the clock as everyone in class collectively holds a breath. The tiniest of the three hands ticks quickly to three thirty, and I wish for more time as everyone else stampedes to the exit.

I now walk home to delay my return by thirty minutes, which gives me more time to lock away the "school" me. Mother was home early the first day and questioned where I was. I told her that I walked to lose weight, which was the lie I knew had the greatest possibility of keeping me out of trouble. Satisfied, she allowed me to continue.

Thus, I return to my prison, where I often tire of being caged and helpless. Red *X*s graffiti my wall calendar as I count down the days to graduation and my eighteenth birthday. I've held on this long, but I don't know if I can make it to the end.

CHAPTER 24

REFLECTION

Sometimes I'm brave. Just brave enough to really look beyond a few stolen glances. Curiosity wins when I change clothes, and I see my reflection in the rectangular mirror hanging on my bedroom wall. *Am I what Mother says?*

Then I chicken out and move closer to the mirror to examine my face. I wish my nose was more like Mother's nose. I wish my eyes were her color blue. Other than our shared complexion and freckles, I look nothing like her. None of us do. My siblings and I have different shades of brown eyes and hair. *Maybe if we did, we wouldn't remind her of Father so much, and she would love us more.*

I've always felt out of place. The vast majority of my world is black or white. I know a few Asian people, but when you are half, you're something else, something odd, something which doesn't belong. I hate being a half breed, a mutt—or at least that's what other people say I am, as if being half of anything makes me tainted. I've been referred to as a Jap, a Chink, and a gook. I don't even know what those mean.

Outside of my siblings, Andrew is the only other mixed person I know, but whereas he looks like a super tall Mexican dude, I apparently stick out. There's no avoiding the commentary or questions. I'm constantly asked, "What are you?"

Human. Female. Tired of people trying to figure out what I am. I don't even know. Why can't I be like everyone else?

When I was little, I told other kids I was white and denied anything to the contrary, despite them calling me a liar. Now, I tell people that my father is Filipino, and I get either a "hey cool," an "oh," or my personal favorite, "That in China?"

I don't identify as Filipino. When my parents divorced, that part of my culture and heritage vanished. Pride became shame, and I learned to hate what made me different. Yet I still remember the Tagalog words my father and his family taught me. I still remember the delicious food and being blessed by my elders with a hand to my forehead. I still remember my tiny grandmother and her kind face.

Backing away from the mirror, I focus on my middle. *Why couldn't I have the skinny genes like Eric and Jenny? Those two could be twins. Meanwhile, I feel like I was switched at birth.* I have a petite stature and an hourglass figure—at least that's what *Cosmo* magazine says. With a hand on my hip, I try to hide the curve and make my shape straight. *Can't change my bones.*

I turn sideways and poke at the outlines of my ribs and hip bones. I look at my flat belly and suck it in. Only when the muscles scream do I allow them to settle back to normal. *My ass, on the other hand.*

I frown at the round reflection and give her a few pokes. I twist around for a better look, and Mother's voice instantly screams in my head. *No one likes a fat ass! Get moving, Bertha! Fatty, fatty, two-by-four. You fucking lard ass! I can hear your thunder thighs clapping from here! Cow! Whale! Ugly, fat, worthless bitch! Goddamn motherfucking whore! Useless slut!*

I face away from the mirror, unable to control the twitching and clenching as the words echo down into my hollow bones. When they finally fade away, I slowly turn around and grimace to examine my teeth. I fight with a Doritos chip stuck behind the metal and rubber band barricade. *At least I'll have a beautiful smile soon.*

I put on my T-shirt and shorts and avoid eye contact with the hideous creature looking back at me.

CHAPTER 25

REQUESTS

Another April Friday afternoon arrives, and I ride the yellow cheese bus to get home early from school. I stare past my reflection in the window and try not to stress out...

Just need to get through this day. Probably flunked my geometry test. Math sucks! Never enough time to study or catch up on all the basics I've missed from always moving. Constant survival mode at home. Who cares about formulas and equations and...my brain hurts. Barely begun that book for English class, and the essay is due next week, along with that biology project. Tonight, my last night to review for the big test. Got to be there at seven thirty in the morning. Must clean the whole house from top to bottom again. Yesterday's cleaning inspection. My lazy dusting wasn't up to code.

⋏

So here I am, scrubbing a clean toilet and dusting the living room shelves. Why? Because Her Majesty has the inhuman ability to find dirt and remember exactly how everything looks. No way I'm getting caught again. I'm a terrible liar.

When I'm half-finished, she arrives home early.

"Hi, Mom," I say as she shuts the front door.

She looks at me and asks, "Why aren't you finished already?"

"Uh, I came straight home and started cleaning like you told me to. You're home early, and I haven't had enough time to finish."

"Oh, yeah. Okay then," she says and walks into her room.

I continue to dust the shelves and knickknacks. "How was your day? I thought you wouldn't be home till late," I say, testing to see if Dragon Lady is tragically depressed, safely neutral, or a raging hell beast this afternoon.

"Fine. Today was my last day. How was your day?" she asks.

Okay...and apparently today was my last day busing tables at the restaurant on the weekends. So much for having a paycheck. Well, at least she's at neutral. Better try my luck. "Meh. I have a lot of homework to do this weekend, plus tonight is my last night to study for the ACT. It's in the morning, remember?"

"What's with this test?" she asks.

"It's the one I paid for when I couldn't give you money for the electric bill. I have to take it for college. Check-in's at seven thirty at Louisiana College."

"Oh, right. Do you need me to drive you?"

"No. It's just over the railroad tracks."

"Okay. Well you better get moving so you can study," she says with a smile.

"About that, Mom. Why do I have to clean the house every day?" I look at her face, which doesn't change, so I continue, "I mean, I'm dusting, and there's no dust." I show her the cleaning rag, damp with furniture polish.

"What's your point?" she asks calmly.

"Doesn't seem like good use of my time cleaning something that's already clean. Maybe if I clean once or twice a week, I would have more time to do laundry. I could fold and put away your laundry before you get home."

She looks at me with consideration and approaches. Not sure what she will do, I move away from the shelf unit. She runs a finger along a shelf I haven't dusted and examines her finger. "I guess you're right," she says. I check my surprise and keep my face passive. She continues, "Once a week, but the kitchen is every day, and you have to finish everything you have left for today."

"Yes, ma'am!" I say.

"Anything else?" she asks.

"Well, I was wondering if it would be too much…" I hesitate to finish.

"Yes?" she says without a sigh, so I ask, "Can Eric mow the grass from now on? He is a boy after all, and I have lots of stuff to do in here."

"You trust your brother with a lawn mower?"

"And why not? I was mowing the grass at eleven, and he's fourteen already. He can handle one small responsibility."

"Might do him some good. Keep him out of your sister's hair for an hour," she says with a chuckle.

"I'm sure she'd appreciate that," I laugh and decide to go three for three. "Speaking of Jenny, could she clean the kitchen a few nights a week? I would have more time to study. I'm trying to pull up my geometry grade like you want."

"Fine," she says.

"Thanks, Mom!" I give her a hug, and she hugs me back. "That will help me a lot with school."

"It better," she says, with a playfully raised eyebrow and a smile. Before I return to my duties, she moves my hair away from my face and tucks it behind my ear.

Wow! That went better than I ever expected.

When Eric gets home, I show him how to start our broke-ass, rigged lawn mower, and off he goes. I finish my chores and attempt to do some homework, but I'm constantly interrupted by everyone. Mother keeps barging into my room with random tasks she won't do herself. I go through Eric's and Jenny's school folders now while Mother is around, or I'll have to forge her signature.

I manage to read a few chapters of *Wuthering Heights* but give up on Heathcliff's issues because Jenny has issues. I close the book with a sigh and head toward her high-pitched screams and cries of woe. Eric loves to aggravate the hell out her nonstop. *I guess I'm on referee duty tonight as well. I live in a goddamn circus.*

CHAPTER 26
HELLO

In the evening, Andrew surpasses punctual, and the phone rings early. He said he'd call to make sure I eat a good meal and go to bed early for the test.

"Hello," I say and get a cheerful hello in return. "What do you want, Andrew?" I tease with annoyance.

"Andrew? Who's Andrew?"

"Oh. I'm sorry! I was expecting someone else."

"Really?"

"Yes. Sorry. Who's this?" I say, embarrassed.

"You don't know who I am?"

"Uh...no. Should I?"

"Yes!" he answers.

"I know your voice, but..." I stop to think. "Well, you're not Reggie or Jake. Who are you?"

Mother comes into the living room and looks at me. I shrug my shoulders.

"Tina, it's me," he says and then asks, "Who are Reggie and Jake?"

"Who is this?" I ask, with real annoyance at the guessing game.

"Someone who loves you," he says quietly.

"*Jon*! Oh my God!" I yell, feeling like an idiot, and see Mother roll her eyes. "I'm so sorry! I can't believe I did that! Oh my God! How are you? Are you home? Are you coming over?" I pull the whole phone into my room, careful not to wrap the long wall cord around the coffee table.

"No," he says sadly. "How could you not know it was me?"

"I'm sorry. I haven't seen you in such a long time, and we haven't talked in over six months, and I have a lot going on and…"

He interrupts me. "Who's Andrew and Reggie and Jake?"

"Oh, I go to school with Andrew. He's my best friend and nothing more. I wrote you that in one of my letters. I was expecting him to call."

"Yes. I remember now."

"Reggie is my older brother from my Dad's first marriage, and Jake is his best friend. They live in Chicago. I was there last month over spring break, and they call me every once in a while."

"You went to Chicago?"

"Yeah, it was awesome!" After I explain the court order, I describe the exhilaration of flying for the first time and how I had Eric convinced to hold on to the bathroom handle or get sucked out of the airplane when the toilet flushes. I talk about the tearful reunion at the gate and the awkwardness of meeting Father's young wife and my two-year-old sister. I describe some of my favorite Filipino foods and help Jon pronounce Filipino words. I tell him all about the late nights hanging out with Reggie and his friends, who teased me about my Southern accent.

When I finish, Jon remembers, "Oh, that's right. I was home that week you were gone. I came over to surprise you."

"Yeah, Mother told me you showed up in uniform. She said you looked handsome. I was so disappointed."

"Me too. I miss you so much," he says.

"And I miss you. I'm sorry about not…"

"Don't worry about it. I didn't realize it's been so long since we've talked. Did you get my letters?"

"Yes. I read them a million times. I'm glad you finally sent me a picture. Did you get all of mine?"

"Yes. They were waiting for me when I got back. I would have called sooner, but your number changed a bunch of times, and I didn't have your newest one until I finished reading the last letter." He sighs. "I wish I could be there to see your face…and the braces."

I giggle. "Oh, sure. I'd probably bite you trying to kiss you."

"I wouldn't mind," he chuckles.

⼈

About half an hour later, Mother opens my bedroom door to tell me it's time to start dinner. I nod my head, and she leaves my door open behind her, so I leave my little couch to close it.

"Jon, I have to go. I need to make dinner, and I have that test tomorrow I need to finish reviewing for."

"No, wait. I have so much more to tell you. Shit. Um. I'll be gone for nine months this time. Out of the country again. I don't know when I'll be able to talk to you. I'll write when I can." He's quiet for a moment before he asks, "You still love me?"

"Of course I do," I tell him.

"And you'll still wait for me?"

"If you wait for me," I reply.

"I will," he says, but I know the possibilities.

"Jon, let's be honest. You're so far away and gone for long periods of time. I know there have been other women."

He hesitates. "Tina, they meant nothing to me. I love you."

Oh, that hurts, but there's nothing I can do about it. Thus is life. "I know. I know you do, and it's okay. It's just the nature of our circumstances. It's hard on both of us." He doesn't say anything more, so I continue, "I really do love you, and I'll try my best. That's all I can promise."

"I know," he says.

Mother yells my name for the third time. "Jon, I really have to go."

"I hate saying goodbye."

"Me too," I say, always wishing we had more time.

"Tina, I love you. Don't forget."

"I won't. I love you, Jonathan. Be safe."

"I will. Bye."

"Bye."

My door flies open. "Didn't you fucking hear me calling your name?" she yells at me.

And there's the Dragon Lady. So much for her good mood. Vinny's not here tonight to calm her down. "Yes, yes. Sorry," I say and move away from her.

"Is he going to show up here tonight?" she asks.

"No, ma'am."

"Good. He's a grown man in the military. Probably out banging every whore he can find. Why he even bothers with your ugly ass, I'll never know."

I control the hurt and anger on my face and say nothing, because I know better. I need to get through the evening without an incident.

CHAPTER 27

Pickles

I choose tuna fish sandwiches and mac and cheese for dinner because they're quick and easy to make. I half pay attention to what I'm doing as the looping conversation with Jon takes over my brain. Mother enters the kitchen with knotted eyebrows, but before she can say anything, I mix the fish and Miracle Whip faster and tell her it will be a few more minutes.

"Hurry it up," she orders.

Before she leaves, I ask, "Can Jenny clean up tonight so I can study?"

"No. You should have thought of that before you wasted all your time on the goddamn phone," she yells on her way back to the living room.

Jesus Christ! She can't be nice for more than three hours? I have so much to do! She keeps me so busy, and then there's all the interruptions every damn day. The math. I'm not going to do well tomorrow. And I have to work tomorrow. Did I wash my uniform? No. Yes. Wait. She quit. She must have my paycheck. Stupid Wuthering Heights. *I hate that book, but I have to finish and write a stupid report about love and… Jon. Nine freaking months. I'm going to go spastic.*

I bring everyone's drinks to the living room and set them on the coffee table. Mother is on the couch with Eric next to her, and Jenny is on the floor at one end of the table. Eric and Jenny thank me. Mother's eyes leave the television for an annoyed glance in my direction.

Quick as flashing paparazzi, I'm back and forth between the kitchen and the living room. Her food is top priority, so she gets her plate first. I make myself a sandwich and eat it as I make my siblings' plates. Once I drop off their food, I'm back in the kitchen, where I take a bite out of the last half of my sandwich. With a spoonful of mac and cheese hovering over my plate, I freeze when I hear Mother scream, "Tina Marie!"

What did I do? Please no. Not tonight. I instantly swallow the mostly chewed sandwich bite and realize what I did. She stomps my way. The beast enters, knocks the sandwich out of my hand, and rages in my face, "You put pickle relish in the tuna fish! *Again*!"

"I'm sorry! I didn't mean to. I…I was supposed to make a separate batch. I guess I wasn't paying attention when—"

"You fucking stupid idiot! You can't ever do a goddamn thing right!" She goes on belittling me, her repertoire of fat and ugly insults vast and powerful.

I panic as the whole day comes crashing down upon me. I can't control myself and scream back at her, "I have enough to do around here. If you don't like it, then fucking make dinner yourself!"

She pops me in the mouth. My eyes water, and my lips sting. I turn to go to my room, but she grabs my upper arm and picks up the pot from the stove.

I cringe and hold my free arm up because I think she will hit me. Instead, she dumps the rest of the family-sized mac and cheese on my head and throws the pot. Orange noodles scatter across the kitchen floor. She slings me toward the pot and into the lower cabinets by the sink.

I turn in time to take the impact with my shoulder. She yells at me to get up, but I remain unmoved as my brain tries to catch up with my body. She stomps a foot in my direction and yells through clenched teeth, "Get the fuck up right now!"

I slowly turn over and sit up. My hands are covered in squashed noodles, and several in perfect form dangle from the web of my hair.

"Look at me!" she orders, so I look at her mouth. "Look me in the eyes when I'm talking to you!" she spits.

My eyes hold the full brunt of her violence and malice.

"Now clean it up!" she barks.

"You clean it up! You made the mess! I'm not cleaning up anything!" I yell right back.

"Oh, yes, you will. Or I won't let you sleep tonight!"

My defiance collapses into tears.

"That's what I thought," she says with a smirk and goes back to the living room.

CHAPTER 28
NUMB

Snap. Snap. Snap. Only I can hear the breaking as my sobs bounce around the kitchen. I slip into the numb hollowness of zombie mode and become silent. I feel nothing and follow orders like a good soldier.

In the pot next to me, three tiny noodles continue to hold on for dear life. On hands and knees, I clean up the rest and retrieve what's left of my sandwich. The garbage can gobbles the ruined food. I want to crawl in and join them, but I spot mop the floor instead.

Scrub, scrub, scrub, scrub, scrub. The dishes look at me, confused no doubt, as I hold them under water long after they are clean. More appear, but I don't notice until Eric and Jenny shut the kitchen door. The constant replay resumes—my skull almost bashing into the cabinets to my lower left. My prune hands are motionless in the dirty, soapy water. I look around and see there's nothing left, so I watch the water disappear and leave the bubbles to defiantly surround the drain.

In the bathroom, I pick the forgotten noodles out of my hair and turn on the shower. I stretch my tender shoulder in the hot, steamy water. *Hello, shoulder. You've never been bruised before. Welcome to the parade. Wear those black and purple and blue colors proudly before they change to green and yellow and disappear.*

I blow-dry my hair until I realize it's been dry awhile, and I'm only staring at the wraith. I leave her know-it-all smirk and open the door to find Mother with tears in her eyes. *And now I have to deal with sad, depressed Mother. I can't even have a pity party to myself.*

"If you would just listen to me and follow directions, I wouldn't have to act like that. Why do you make me do that?" she says and tries to hug me.

I push past her and say, "Stay away from me."

She cries even more. I shut my bedroom door in her face and sit by my closet. *I don't care anymore.*

"Tina, open the door so we can talk."

"No, Mother, go away."

She cries more, and the more she cries, the angrier I become.

"Tina, please."

"Just leave me alone!"

"Tina Marie, open the door," she says, and I yell louder, "Or what? You'll pour more food on me?"

"Open this door right now, or I'll…"

"What? What will you do? What more could you possibly do to me? Go ahead, kick in the door! Rip it off the hinges!"

"Tina, I love you."

"I don't care! *I don't care!*" I scream at the top of my lungs, "You are a terrible mother! You're vile and wicked, and I hope you burn in hell! I don't care what you do to me anymore! I don't care!"

"Why would you say that to me?" she sobs, and her footsteps disappear into her room.

I cry and laugh and scream, "Because I hate you!" I open my closet door and lob a shoe at our shared bedroom wall. The result tickles my rage. Shouts of "I hate you!" announce each volley as I throw another and another, harder and harder. Boom, boom, boom, boom, boom, boom, boom.

Out of ammunition after four pairs, my scattered shoes and I remain silent. *There's no one. No Jonathan to stop the bleeding. No Jackie returning from exile to stop the drowning. God does not hear my pain and sorrows. Alone.*

Out of habit, I rock back and forth until my breaths are no longer ragged, and the tears have dried where they fell. I return my shoes to the closet and crawl up to bed to set my alarm clock. One thirty looks at me with pity. I pull the ceiling chain that is tied to my bed railing, and the light says good night with a click. In the darkness, I contemplate the least painful ways to commit suicide.

⋏

Andrew, cheerful as usual, sees me at the end of the line and moves from his place two people ahead of me.

"Hey," he says and steps behind me. "I kept moving back to wait for you. I thought you weren't going to make it."

"Well, I did. I got up late."

"I called you last night, but your mom said you were busy."

"I was," I say.

"Did you eat a good breakfast? Today is going to be a long day."

"Nope."

"Then why didn't you call me? I could have brought you some donuts."

I don't say anything as he looks me over. He continues, "What's wrong?"

"Nothing," I reply.

"It's seventy-something degrees outside. Why are you wearing a sweater, and what's with the sunglasses?"

"I don't feel good. I may have the flu."

"You were fine yesterday."

"Just drop it, Andrew. I want to get this over with."

"Tina, what happened? Did something happen with your mom?"

I don't answer, because the lady calls me forward a second time. He places a hand on my arm and says, "Wait."

"Good luck," I say and shrug away to be processed.

About five minutes into instructions, I'm sweating to death. I avoid looking in Andrew's direction two seats away to my left. After we begin the test, I shift my sunglasses to the top of my head after a proctor tells me I can't wear them. Since I finally have enough with my face melting, I take off my sweater and hang it on the back of my chair. As I face forward, I see Andrew's eyes on my arm and stare right back at him with exposed, puffy eyes. The proctor walks by and asks, "Is there a problem here?"

We both answer no.

I take my time. Andrew is one of the first people to leave. He's nowhere to be found when I'm the second-to-last person to finish. I walk home alone.

CHAPTER 29

Almost

I've had a hell of a week since the pickle relish incident. First, Mother didn't talk to me for two glorious days. Then, she took my door completely off the hinges. It stands ready on the back porch, a portal to nowhere. Finally, her incessant insults began, tormenting me whenever we occupy the same area or when she walks by the missing piece of my room.

⋏

Nope. Slicing or stabbing myself is out. Too painful...although I could make a spectacular bloody mess all over her room before I check out. Playing in traffic involves other people, and that's not nice. Someone else would get hurt. Could easily walk to the bridge over the river and jump off. It might be high enough. If I don't die from the impact, drowning and eaten by alligators...um, no thank you. Too public anyway. Someone would try to stop me.

Today, I have the solution and enter the bathroom. I open the mirror above the sink, and there they stand—about two dozen orange prescription bottles lining two shelves.

Mother always has some kind of sleepy pain meds, but which one? I turn the bottles so the directions and warnings face me. I skim for keywords. *Oh, here. These three will do.* Luckily, they are all half full.

I'm pretty small, with low tolerance. Maybe fifteen or twenty? Should I take them all? Mother goes to work tonight and will be gone till Sunday. Better get a big glass of water then go to bed after everyone else is asleep. Is that the phone ringing again? Where is everybody? I better answer it, or she'll wake up early, and that's never good.

I quickly put the bottles in place on the shelves and shut the cabinet. As I quietly run to the living room, I listen for movement from her room. I answer the phone and hear Jon's voice.

"I thought you were gone already," I say.

"I'm leaving in three days. I was able to come home first. I bought a new car, and I'm coming over right now."

"That's not a good idea. My mom's in a mood. She leaves for work in an hour, so come over in an hour and a half to make sure she's gone."

"So, we'll be alone?" he asks.

"No, my brother and sister, remember?" I remind him.

"Right."

"Better yet, why don't you pick me up, and we can go on a proper date."

"Tina, you're not seventeen yet. She's not going to let me, no matter how many times we ask."

"I know that. She started working long shifts last weekend all the way in Marksville. Since it's Saturday, she doesn't come home till Sunday afternoon or evening, so I'm free."

"You mean you're going to sneak out? Are you serious? That's not like you."

"Desperate times call for desperate measures," I say and hope he won't refuse.

"Okay then. Where do you want to go?"

"I don't know. The mall? The movies? I don't really care. I just need to see you and get out of this house."

"Tina, are you okay? You don't sound like yourself."

"I'm fine. Just be here in an hour and a half."

⊥

Mother leaves exactly an hour later. I tell Eric and Jenny that I'm going out with Jon, and I don't know when I'll be back. They can fend for themselves while I'm gone. Jenny is twelve. I watched four kids at that age, but I convince Eric not to leave her. There's a fifty-fifty chance he'll keep his promise.

In a chair by the front window, I stare at the street. *This wasn't part of my plan. Should I tell Jon what happened?* My eyes water as I think about that conversation, but I refuse to ruin my makeup.

A black sports car replaces my view of the concrete road, but the change doesn't register until I see Jon. I rush out the door. He has a big smile on his face and says, "Hey, beautiful!"

Ignoring the "beautiful" remark, I tackle him around the chest before he even gets halfway to the door. He picks me up and takes a deep breath. When he sets me down, I refuse to let him go. *Loved and safe.*

"I know you missed me, but you don't have to squeeze me to death." He laughs. I release my hold and look up at him. "Now, don't cry. We've only just said hello," he says and wipes a tear from my cheek. "How are we going to get through saying goodbye? Come on, let me see that smile. I want a good look at those braces."

I laugh and give him a grin. Cupping my chin, he turns my face from side to side. "Adorable," he says and kisses me gently, as if to test out the feel of the braces, then desperately and hungrily as we wrap up in each other's arms. I can't control the tears. He ends the kiss, and we wipe my tears off each other's faces.

"There, there," he says, "See, you didn't even bite me."

He always knows how to make me laugh. We walk to the car, and I apologize, "I'm sorry I'm such a blubbering mess."

"Well, pull yourself together, woman. We've got a date to go on," he teases and opens the car door for me.

When he doesn't turn toward Alexandria, I ask, "Where are we going?"

"First, there's a stretch of highway without any cops. I'm itching to see how fast this baby can go."

⋏

We drive out past Tioga. Jon holds my hand and talks about his adventures along the way. I try to listen, but my mind wonders. I think about what happened last week and…

What if Jenny is all alone? What if Mother comes home early? What will happen if she does? Should I tell Jon everything? Is midnight the right time to drink all those pills? What will that do to him?

I barely notice when we drive down a stretch of straight highway, U-turn, and drive back the direction we came from before U-turning again.

Jon says, "All's clear," and I realize we are stopped on the road. "Better put your seatbelt on," he says, and when I follow his instructions, he asks, "Ready?"

"Yep," I reply.

He checks his rearview mirror. "Brace yourself."

I lean back, and he floors it. The wheels spin for a moment, and we shoot forward. *This must be what ludicrous speed feels like!*

Jon yells, "*Woooo!*" as we zoom up to ninety and right past the fifty-mile-per-hour sign.

"Holy shit, that was fast!" I exclaim, my heart pumping.

We slow, U-turn, and speed down the highway at just over one hundred. I hold on to the "oh, shit" handle as he takes the next U-turn fast and speeds up in the straightaway.

A police siren wails behind us.

My daredevil groans, "*Fuuuuuck!*" as he pulls onto the shoulder.

After examining Jon's license, registration, and insurance, the officer asks, "So, son, out for a little joyride?"

"Yes, sir. Just got the car today."

The officer looks at me, then back at Jon. He sighs and says, "I'm letting you go with a warning."

"Thank you, sir," Jon says with relief.

"But the joyride is over. Understand?" he says sternly.

"Yes, sir," Jon answers.

Before he hands over Jon's license, the officer says, with a wink at me, "And take your girl somewhere nice."

Jon smiles and glances at me. "Will do, sir."

We sit in complete silence until the officer drives away.

"That was close," Jon says and takes my hand.

"Yep," I agree.

He studies my face, and I see the concern. "What's wrong?" he asks.

"I have a lot on my mind," I answer and look out the window, away from scrutiny and suspicion. The sun is just low enough to blind me, so I flip down the visor.

"Don't evade the question. You know that doesn't work with me. What is going on? You're not yourself. You sneak out, and you've said all of ten words since you got in the car."

I stay silent, and he jiggles our linked hands. I look back at him, but he's focused on the fading bruise decorating my left shoulder. He lets go of my hand and raises my short sleeve.

"What happened to your arm?"

"Nothing to worry about," I tell him.

"Did your mom do that?" he asks, but I refuse to answer. "Jesus Christ, Tina!" he shouts. "When are you going to stop taking her shit? You told me she doesn't hit you anymore! Why don't you call someone, get some help?"

"Please don't yell! I can't take anymore yelling!" I say, fighting the tears.

"Tina, she can't treat you like that!" he continues at a lower volume. "I should call the cops or just go over there myself and…"

"No! Don't do that!" I shout and ball my eyes out. "She's crazy, and you'll end up with more than a warning from the police!" I cover my face with my hands.

I hear him blow out a long breath, and then his seat moving back. He takes both of my hands and says, "Come here." He pulls me onto his lap and cradles me like a little kid. "Don't cry. I'm sorry. I'm not angry at you." With his face against my hair, he continues, "It will be okay."

When I calm down, I say, "Jon, I can't. I can't do the police and social services, lawyers and courts. My only alternative is to leave everything I have, again, and move to Chicago. This is the longest I've ever been in one place, and I just want to finish high school. Then, I'll be eighteen and on my own."

He wipes away the lingering tears and then kisses the areas of my face where all the fear existed. When he's done, I watch his contemplative face, but he says nothing more, so I remind him, "She's not bad all the time." I snuggle into his chest and listen to his heartbeat until he finally says, "Tina…I don't like it, but I won't do anything. If she bruises you again, call the cops."

"I will," I say and hope he'll be satisfied, but he turns my face to his and kisses me lightly on the lips.

I open my eyes, and he says, "Promise me."

"I promise," I tell him, without flinching from his gaze. *The guilt for the lie won't matter soon enough anyway.*

He looks at me for a long moment. "Let me take you home," he says and releases me.

"Oh. Okay," I say, confused, and crawl back into the passenger seat. With his seat back in place, his hand surrounds mine, and he explains, "I'll take you home. To my house. My mother wants to meet you before she leaves for vacation tonight. I'll cook dinner, and then we can be alone. You can spend the night, and I'll take you home in the morning before your mom gets there."

I look at him as the words sink in. "That's a big decision. I can't even think right now," I say.

"Tina, there's no pressure. It's just a suggestion."

"I don't have clothes or anything."

"I have everything you could need. Extra toothbrush. You can even take a shower. I'll give you one of my T-shirts to sleep in, if you'd like."

"Do you have protection?" I ask.

"Yes," he answers and waits.

I look at the highway stretched out before us and flip up the visor now that the sun is obscured by trees. I think about what will happen if I accept his offer—both of us in the shower, then in his bed, how we will fall asleep wrapped around each other, and…how all of it will completely ruin my plan.

I finally look at him and say, "Jon, I love you, and as much as I want to be with you like that, I can't. Not yet, you know that. You're leaving, and I won't see you for like nine months or whatever. I'm sorry."

He kisses my hand and gives me a half smile before saying, "It's okay. You know I understand."

"Yes, thank you," I say, with my free hand to one side of his face.

"Well, what would you like to do now?" he asks and pulls back onto the highway.

I sigh and say, "Just take me home. I shouldn't have left my sister alone. Eric probably ditched her."

"Are you sure?"

"Yes. So much for our big date," I say and silently hold his hand in my lap all the way back to prison.

Jon turns the corner, and we see Mother's car parked in the driveway.

"Fuck!" I say, "Good thing I came home."

I imagine the humiliating temper tantrum and start to freak out, but Jon squeezes my hand and says, "I'll talk to her. She seems to like me. Don't worry."

We park in front of the mailbox. I jump out and go directly to Mother's car. I place a hand on the metal hood and tell a confused Jon, "It's still hot. Must have just got home. Within twenty minutes, tops."

Mother opens the front door before I can get up the porch steps. Wrath dances in her eyes and instantly vanishes when she sees Jon step up from behind me.

"Hello!" he says cheerfully, with a big smile to match. I glance from him to her and watch that warm, deceptive smile appear on her face.

"Hello, Jonathan," she says with the predictable, sugary sweet fake voice I know so well.

My eyes want to roll, but fear keeps them in check. I watch as her eyes rake him over. *You got to be kidding me! Like a lioness sizing up its prey.*

"Didn't know you were home," she drawls.

"Oh yes, ma'am. Just for a few days. I came by to visit and show off my new car." He gestures behind us. Her gaze moves to the car. "Do you like it?" he asks with a boyish grin. *Oooh, he's laying on the charm real thick. Dangerous games we play. Hope it works.*

Without even a glance at me, she walks past us to take a closer look. I barely breathe as I stay rooted where I am and watch them. Mother travels clockwise to inspect every angle, and Jon proudly tells her all about it as he follows. When she sticks her head in the open driver's side window, I move closer and stop by the mailbox.

"She's a beauty," Mother comments.

"Much like your daughter," he says and gives me a wink. She laughs. Inside I flinch, but I keep a smile plastered on my face until Jon's eyes return to the car.

Her curiosity satisfied, she makes her way back to me and asks, "And what have you two been up to?"

Jon joins us, takes my hand, and answers for me, "Oh, I'm sorry about that. It's my fault." He moves me slowly behind him as he says, "I surprised her about twenty minutes or so ago and took her out for a spin."

When she doesn't immediately react, I move around him so I can check her face. He glances at me and moves closer so that he's standing directly in front of her. He continues, "I know we shouldn't have, since you weren't home to ask, but I can be charming and all." He shrugs his shoulders and grins down at her.

She smiles back and croons, "I can see that." Her eyes slide over to me. "Is that true?"

I look her right in the eyes. "Yes, ma'am. We just drove around the neighborhood. He went a little too fast and almost got a ticket. Otherwise, we would have been back sooner."

"Boys and their toys," she laughs and pats his upper arm. Ignoring me, she saunters past, and I get a glimpse of her pleased face.

My eyes focus on Jon as he watches her go up the steps. Her footsteps disappear into the house. I don't dare turn around, even after the front door closes.

"Oh my God! That was close," I say and let out a held breath. Time catches up with itself, and I realize that darkness has begun to consume the world.

"Your mother's a real piece of work," he says with a tense face. His eyes continue to watch the door.

"You have no idea. At least she likes you."

"Yeah, a little too much," he says and shakes his head.

"I'm sorry," I say, mortified.

He instantly traps me within a tight embrace. "It's not your fault. Fourteen more months, and you'll be free."

Unable to move, I mutter into his chest, "Yeah, that's the plan."

He puts his hands on both sides of my face and peers down at me. "I don't know how you can stand it. Are you sure you don't want me to do something?"

"Yes, I'm sure. I'll be all right. It's not for much longer."

Seemingly content with my reassurances, he kisses me, and our arms wrap around each other. I'm thankful for the chance to see him and to say goodbye. When the long kiss ends, he holds me close and says, "I love you. Always and forever," to which I instinctively reply, "No matter what."

Our words echo in my head. "Wait. What did you just say?" I ask, unable to move.

"I love you always and forever…no matter what. I like that," he answers and repeats it all together, "I love you always and forever, no matter what."

My fingers grip his shirt as my eyes water.

He looks down at me and says, "Oh, please don't cry, or I won't leave you here tonight. We still have tomorrow and Monday after you get out of school. I can come pick you up."

I let him go, but his fingers wrap around my right hand, and he says, "Call me, and let me know if she'll let me and what time."

"Thank you, and I'm sorry," I say, with utmost sincerity.

"You have nothing to be sorry for. You better go in. She's watching us."

He kisses my forehead, and we say goodbye. I sit at the top of the porch steps and wave as he drives away.

Five seconds later, I hear the front door open. Like a ghost, cigarette smoke surrounds me. I watch the white tendrils vanish into the wind before I continue to stare down the road. Dusk darkens the world further.

"I take it he wants to come over for the next few days," Mother says.

"Yes, ma'am. And if it's all right, can he pick me up from school on Monday? We will come straight home. I'll be here before the bus could drop me off."

"Hmm…well, you're lucky I like him, especially after the stunt you pulled this evening."

"Does that mean he can?"

"Yes," she answers, before saying sarcastically, "Who am I to deny true love?"

"Thanks, Mom," I say, with a glance in her direction.

"But only when I'm home, and no more running off alone with him. You won't be seventeen for another two months. You understand?"

"Yes, ma'am," I reply, and since it is safe to continue, I ask, "You're really going to hold me to our agreement until then?"

She laughs. "Yes, no dates for two months."

Well, our negotiated bargain is better than the original "not until you're eighteen."

"I better start lining them up," I say and watch her facial expression change from shock to worry to panic. "Mom, don't have a heart attack. I'm just kidding. You'll be happy to know there's no one else."

A shrill ring interrupts our conversation, and she runs into the house to answer the phone. I sit where I am in the dark and try to ignore the words that echoed in my head earlier. For once, I doubt my plan, and I think about Jon and our crazy afternoon together.

Will he blame himself for not intervening? Who will be the one to tell him when he calls? Will he arrive to see them pull my body out of the house? Will he drive himself mad replaying our last day together over and over? Will he ever understand why? They won't find a note. I want that bitch to suffer through questions and the police and the coroner and the funeral. Ah, but she'll put on a good act and get sympathy, but at least I'll be free. I may burn in hell, but I'd rather take my chances there.

The porch light unexpectedly brightens my world. The door opens, and Mother says with a laugh, "Tina, what are you still doing out here? Waiting for the pizza in the dark? I didn't even see you go out."

I look at her and force myself to smile. "You look pretty. Going out?" I ask.

"Yes," she answers, and her high heels click down the steps past me. "Dinner should be here any minute. The money is on the coffee table. Don't wait up."

"Have fun," I say as she slams the car door, and off she goes.

⋏

After dinner, I dial Jon's number. *If he comes back, I won't go through with it. Maybe. At least not until after he's gone.*

"Hello, sweetheart," his mother says after I say hello and ask for him.

Byron. He's the only one who calls me sweetheart. I haven't been allowed to see him since he drove Father to the airport. It's not the lawyers' or the judge's fault Father got out of jail early. Just another of Mother's excuses to keep me away from someone else who loves me, or anyone normal, for that matter.

"He's not home. I thought he was out with you," she says.

"He was, but I had to come back home. I thought you were going on vacation."

"I am. I leave in a little bit, but I was hoping I could finally meet you before I left."

"Oh, I'm sorry. My mother came home and…"

"Oh, no. I'm the one that feels sorry for you. She's really going to hold you to it. Your mother is one tough cookie."

"You could call her that," I say.

"Well, there's always next time. We'll get to see a lot of each other when Jon gets back."

"Yes, I suppose so."

"You two are going to stick it out," she states.

"Yes, ma'am. We're trying to."

"I know. It's hard. Just be patient. He really does love you."

"I know he does. Thank you for being so kind. Enjoy your vacation."

"I will. Hey, ya know, he's probably over at Nick's. Lord knows he has to show off that car."

I laugh. "Yes, so true."

"Want Nick's number?"

"Sure, and can you leave him a note just in case I can't get a hold of him? He can come over tomorrow."

She gives me the number and says, "Alright, honey. You take care now."

"You too, and thank you."

Great. Now his mother will be the last adult I speak to unless I actually call Nick.

⸸

Nick answers the phone, and I hear a bunch of people in the background.

"Hey, Nick. It's me, Tina. How are you?"

"Hi! Great! Hold on a sec," he says and yells away from the phone, "Jon, it's Tina!"

I hear a bunch of guys whistle, make kissing noises, and yell comments. From a distance, Jon says, "Shut up, assholes."

I can't help but laugh when they don't.

When he gets to the phone, he says, "Hi! How did you find me?"

"I called your house and talked to your mom for a while. She gave me Nick's number, and here we are."

"Are you okay?"

"Yeah, my mom went out and won't be back until tomorrow. I thought…"

I'm interrupted by what sounds like scuffling, and then Marcus yells into the phone, "He *looooves* you!" followed by Jon saying, "Don't be a dick!" The group starts chanting my name, and I crack up.

"All of you! Assholes! My God!" he yells at them before saying to me, "Sorry about that. You were saying?"

"Have y'all been drinking?" I ask, still laughing.

"Some more than others. I wish you were here. There's a bonfire and everything."

"Me too. Sounds like a good time," I say and become silent. I imagine all the fun they're having and how I always miss out on everything because I'm trapped in this house, being a tormented slave.

"Tina?" he says, which pulls me from my misery, and I continue, "Anyway, as I was saying, I thought you could come back while she's gone, but you're busy."

"Yeah, since I couldn't be with you, I came over to Nick's, and everyone showed up, and it turned into a party. I can come back."

I hear "aw" and "boo" in the background. "No, that's okay, especially if you've been drinking," I say and refuse to reveal my disappointment.

"I'm fine. I haven't had much."

"No, stay with your friends. Have fun."

"Are you sure? I can be there in twenty minutes."

"You can come over tomorrow. I suspect you'll be hung over, so call me when you wake up."

"I will. Thanks. I love you."

I hear a bunch of cheering and a chorus of "bye, Tina" and "love you, Tina" in the background.

"Tell those drunkards I said hello. I love you too."

Midnight. I sit at the top of my loft bed ladder and hold my alarm clock. Eric and Jenny are fast asleep, and I'm in my pajamas. I debated all evening about what to do, and I make my decision now that time is up.

In the kitchen, I open a cabinet and look at the mishmash of cups and glasses. I choose a large, plastic purple-and-yellow LSU cup and go to the bathroom. Once my assistant is half-filled with water, I remove the pill bottles from their home behind the mirror. I close the cabinet and stare at myself as I have second thoughts. I stare at the bottles waiting unquestionably on the side of the little porcelain sink. The debate continues until I decide to relive all the mean and nasty things Mother has ever said or done to me. Afterward, my heart hardens…

I am worthless and ugly and fat and unloved. I hate myself for letting her do this to me. I deserve to be punished for letting her do this to me, for being broken and weak.

I see each incarnation of the wraith in the mirror, with their various placements of bruises and cuts and scrapes. I see the fading bruise on my arm. I see the hopelessness on my face.

I don't care anymore. I don't matter, and I don't care. Maybe she will finally feel some real guilt, but it doesn't matter. I just want it all to end. To sleep and never ever hear that voice again. Peaceful darkness, I welcome you.

With easy twists, the bottles open, and I pour as much as I can of each into the palm of my left hand. The giant hill staring back at me is difficult to contain.

I think of Eric and Jenny. *Squirmy Eric looking up at me from the basinet. To the question of what I thought, I answered, "He looks like trouble." I was right. He was the master of mess and breaking toys. We fought* like cats and dogs until Jenny was old enough to pick on, and we convinced her to eat a mud pie.

Waiting in the front window on the day Jenny came home the hospital. Father carried her into the house as I jumped up and down to get a glimpse. Tiny feet sticking out of the blue and pink blanket my grandmother had crocheted. Her smiling face and chubby hands when I helped change her diaper.

They were mine, and I was theirs from the moment I saw them. I tried to take care of them. Protect them. I hope they will be okay without me. They should understand the most.

I think of Andrew. *It was nice to have a best friend again, even for a small while. He knows so little about what happens around here. He will understand the least.*

I think of Jon. *I'm grateful to have had him in my life, even in those brief, shiny ripples here and there, but it's not enough love and affection to sustain this life. He will be the one who suffers the most. I hope one day he will forgive me. Didn't really feel our last kiss. Haven't felt much of anything this week. Any fleeting feelings return to emptiness.*

I pick up the cup and think of our words to each other and how they echoed in my head.

"I love you. Always and forever."

"No matter what."

I hear our voices as I relive that moment several times, but then Jon's voice changes to an older man's voice, full of absolute love and affection, and my voice shifts to my childlike voice of long ago.

"Sweetheart, I love you. And no matter how old you are or where you are or what happens, never forget that you are loved, always and forever…"

"*...no matter what.*"

I hear my tiny voice finishing Byron's sentence like I always do, for as long and as far back as I can remember. I look from the pills to the wraith in the mirror. "You are loved," I whisper to her tear-streaked face.

You are loved. You are loved. You are loved.
You are loved! You are loved! You are loved!
You are loved!
You are loved!
You are loved!

A lost place inside me burns white-hot and melds many shattered pieces back together. I take a deep breath, and like a rubber band, I snap back to life. "What am I doing?" I say out loud. I set the cup on the sink's inner edge, where it balances for a second and then takes a nosedive. I jump back, and the pills go flying. They scatter all over the floor, under the clawfoot tub, and around the base of the sink and toilet. I barely hear their tiny screams over my labored breaths. They bounce around until their colors lie still, in a random display around me.

I rescue the overturned cup and place it firmly on the side of the sink. Squatting, I scoop most of the pills together into a pile. The renegades under the tub by the wall are slightly out of reach, so I lay on my stomach and capture them. I separate them into their respective groups, picking out hair and fuzz as I go. *Too bad for her I didn't clean the bathroom today.*

With one set in my trembling hand, I stand and grab the correct bottle. The sink eats a snack. I look at my determined face in the mirror...

Dammit. I'll have to tell her they spilled down the drain while I was cleaning the cabinet. What to say? "Well, you didn't put the top on all the way, and when I was cleaning the cabinet, they fell in the sink." Good enough.

I kneel to bring the bottles close to the floor. The next two groups fall safely among their brethren. With caps secured, the bottles return to their rightful places, where they pretend to be ignorant of their unsanctioned journeys. After I scrub my hands and face and put the cup in the kitchen drain rack, I lay in bed and press the play button on my remote control. My Weezer CD spins in the boom box my father bought me when I was in Chicago. I fall asleep to "Say It Ain't So."

Throughout every difficulty over the next year or any year thereafter, I never try to take my own life, because I know I am loved no matter what.

CHAPTER 30

TOAST

A slap in the face is, at best, a jarring experience. A slap in the face by a loved one is horrific. Repeated slaps in the face by my own mother…now that shreds places. She seems to enjoy slapping me. She has no remorse in her eyes, nor tears or shreds of decency, no conscience to tell her that violence is wrong.

⟁

I learned to cook out of necessity. Figure out how or starve. I was proud of my efforts, and so was Mother. I had potential. She taught me how to use the appliances, the correct pots and pans, and how to boil water. After we made Kraft Mac and Cheese together, I was on my own. Follow the directions on the back of a box or jar and dump canned food into a pot. Boil and mix. Boil and mix. Always boil and mix.

Cooking was by trial and error or more like trial by fire, depending on Mother's mood. When food was abundant, so was the verbal abuse. When food was scarce, so was she. As I scrounged together meals in peace, I often imagined she was out at fancy restaurants, feasting to her heart's content.

My only reprieve was when Mother wanted McDonald's or pizza or when she felt extra parental. Baked scalloped potatoes with porkchops and fried chicken were her specialties. I groaned every time she announced her intentions. Those evening meals were the messiest, and lucky me had to clean them up. When mustache Jim came around, he made the best meatloaf, pork chops, and skillet-fried steak.

The aroma of those delicious meals led me to the kitchen each time they cooked, until curiosity and the need to please landed this cat with more responsibilities. Since then, when Mother orders the meals, I move about the kitchen with a scowl and take out my frustrations on the food I chop, mash, and mix.

▲

I detest—or better yet, loathe—cooking with absolute certainty, which brings me to Mother's Day. Since I never have money to buy gifts, I make Mother breakfast in bed, if and when she is home. She never deserves to be celebrated, but I always do, despite her random, horrid rottenness. She is still my mother, the only parent I have, and I love her.

Last Mother's Day, she disappeared the night before to party at a bar or some other nonsense. The next morning, she yelled at me when I opened the door and tried to wake her up with pancakes and eggs. My efforts went cold and uneaten into the garbage, along with the innocent plate, fork, and butter knife.

A few weeks after Jon left, Mother's Day sneaks up on me.

From her bedroom, Mother wakes me up by calling my name repeatedly like a broken record with her annoying singsong voice. *Shit. Today is Mother's Day. Was hoping we could somehow skip it this year. As if.*

"What?" I say, taking a deep breath.

"Tina Marie, where's my breakfast? Tina Marie, wake up. It's Mother's Day. I want oatmeal and toast and orange juice. Tina Marie, do you hear me?"

"Yeah, I hear you, you crazy bitch," I say to myself and climb out of bed. The whole time I make her food, I go through every swear word I've ever heard, over and over in my head. *I should spit in her oatmeal.*

Her toast is a little too brown, but I give them to her anyway, hoping she won't care today. *My mistake.* She complains they're burnt, so I put more bread in the toaster and eat the rejects while I wait.

"Hurry up with the toast. I can't eat my oatmeal without it," she calls from her bed.

"I can't make the toaster go any faster, Mother."

And her predicted whining begins. "Where are my other children? Why aren't all my children here with me? Eric. Jenny. Why are my children not giving me love on Mother's Day?"

I go to their rooms. "Get up now before she starts. This day is going to bad enough as it is," I tell them and return to the kitchen. *Dammit. And now I have actual burnt toast because this piece-of-crap toaster has to be watched.* I toss the dead ones and put two more slices in. That's the last of the bread.

"Tina Marie, did you burn the toast?"

"No, that's just me finally burning down the house."

"What was that?" she asks.

"Yes, Mother, I burnt the toast."

"This Mother's Day isn't turning out the way it should. Oh, there's my other children."

"Could they have gone any slower?" I say to myself. I glare at the suspicious toaster and tap, tap, tap my foot. *Let's get this over with so I can go back to bed.*

Finally, the bread turns Mother-approved brown, and I pull up the lever. I butter the toast with the Mother-approved amount and the Mother-approved coverage.

"Tina, you need to warm up my oatmeal, and I need more juice."

I go back into her bedroom, grab the tray, warm up the oatmeal for one minute in our borrowed microwave, stir it up, refill the orange juice, and put everything back on the tray.

"Don't you have anything to say?" she asks as I hand her the tray.

I look at her messy hair and how comfortable she must be propped up by all those pillows. "Happy Mother's Day," I answer.

"What's with the attitude?" she asks in her normal bitchy voice.

"Nothing, I'm just tired," I reply before using a more delightful tone, "Happy Mother's Day!"

"That's better," she says and begins to eat. Eric and Jenny go back to bed. I return to the kitchen to clean up and make myself something else to eat.

Thirty seconds later, her door whooshes open. She yells that her toast is cold and throws them at me. They bounce off my arm because I'm in the middle of pouring milk into a bowl of cereal.

Down at my feet are two perfectly buttered toasts, one with a bite taken out of it. "Well," I say, "if you want more toast, you're gonna have to go to the store to get more and make it yourself."

Surprise, surprise, she slaps me in the face. I tell her I hate her, so she smacks me again. I burn with rage and yell, "Is that all you've got?"

She pops me even harder, but I get in her face and scream, "Hit me! Hit me again!" She pushes me away and does as I command. "Go ahead, keep hitting me! All you do is hit me! Not going to change the fact that I hate you!"

One side of my face is numb, and I laugh despite the tears. Real, burning hate snaps into place, and the smidgeon of love I had left diminishes and disappears. "You," I say, holding my cheek, "you treat me like this! You treat us all like this! You'll get what you deserve!"

"You dare threaten me?" She raises her hand.

"Oh no, Mother. Please. Hit me again." I laugh like a crazy person. She doesn't move, so I say, dead serious with a hate-filled voice, "It doesn't matter, anyway, 'cause in your future, you are going to die old and alone, and no one will mourn you."

She drops her hand, and the color drains from her face. Without a word, she walks into her room and quietly closes the door.

The silent house looks around for high fives. The mush in my bowl cheers and slides into the garbage can with a plop. The fridge nods, and the milk gives me a wink from the cold interior. I return to bed, where I fall asleep with a smile on my face.

CHAPTER 31

HOLIDAYS

How is she going to ruin it? Ah, the million-dollar question that Eric, Jenny, and I ask ourselves. It's pretty much a roll of the dice to see which holiday will be filled with drama and trauma—always my favorite times of the year, when we are stuck at home with her Supreme Being.

Other than the festivities at our schools, we never celebrate Mardi Gras or Valentine's Day, no Memorial or Labor Day barbeques, no Fourth of July fireworks. Those mostly consist of her disappearing to party with her friends. If we are lucky, we visit family or friends.

My siblings and I usually spend New Year's Eve watching television. They fall asleep around eleven, and I watch until the National Anthem comes on, and the channel turns to snow. I ring in the new year saying "Happy New Year" to myself before going to bed.

Thanksgivings are spent at someone else's house, be it family or friends who invite us over for food. Easters consist of egg hunts at church with my grandmother, if she is in town to take us.

For the most part, we only celebrate Christmas and Halloween...well, other than the holy day of mothers and, surprisingly, my birthday. Mother always goes above and beyond for my special day, which I guess is her way of making up for the rest of my miserable life. I usually enjoy Mother's best behavior, a day off, and a party, but they come with a dose of guilt. We never celebrate Eric's or Jenny's birthdays.

Halloween usually involves elaborate outdoor decorations and costumes, and that's only if we have extra money. After my twelfth birthday, I became responsible for trick-or-treating with my siblings. Mother often goes out to a party or bar and leaves us to our own devices.

Christmas is the only holiday we consistently spend together. The living room always smells of pine and popcorn until after New Year's. Every year, Mother comes home with a real tree, and we sing along to radio Christmas carols as we decorate. We wrap it in multicolored lights and a fresh-cooked popcorn garland made by the four of us with needles and thread. Many of the decorations are old and worn, and any new ones are made at school. Mother always stands on a chair to hang the star. With our pooled stash of candy canes from school and work hanging on the ends of the branches, we finish our masterpiece with shiny, metallic strings of tinsel.

Together we admire our work until one of us announces the popcorn-tossing competition. Eric throws a piece in the air, which he tries to catch in his mouth. We eventually toss each other pieces, but Mother wisely ends the game when it turns into Eric throwing popcorn at Jenny.

On Christmas Eves, Mother makes dinner, we watch a movie rented from the video store, and we drink hot chocolate with marshmallows. On Christmas mornings, once everyone is awake, we separate our presents, count to three, and proceed to open them as fast as possible. Wrapping paper flies in every direction as we each exclaim in our own little way the happiness gifts bring.

Our presents are always needed clothes and shoes. They are rarely anything else or extravagant, and when I say extravagant, I mean maybe one or two brand new toys for my siblings and jewelry or makeup for me. Afterward, everyone gets dressed in our new outfits, and we go to a family member's house for lunch or dinner.

⋏

I am seventeen, and I know this Christmas will be our last together, but instead of a stellar holiday to remember, Mother strikes again.

Poor Vinny jumped ship before Thanksgiving, and here we are decorating the tree without Mother, who now works at a hotel less than five miles away. We expect her to come home in the late afternoon, because she called at the end of her shift to say she's on her way and is so excited to decorate the tree. An hour later, she calls to say she's running late and will be home soon. Two hours after that, we get another phone call. She ran into some friends and decided to stay. We could decorate without her.

I hang up the phone and look at the already decorated tree with contempt.

The next day, she comes home to find three upset children. She apologizes for ditching us, promises to never do it again, and treats us to drive-through McDonalds for lunch. We hate McDonalds because we go there all the time. Within the week, she buys me Sasha, a three-year-old Siberian husky with the most beautiful crystal blue eyes.

On Christmas Eve, Mother works her usual shift, and we expect her to return sometime around five o'clock. Thinking that maybe she didn't pay the bill, I check the house phone several times to make sure I get a dial tone. We eat dinner without her. At eight o'clock, I call her work, and they say she left after her shift.

Did she get into an accident? Please, not on Christmas. I don't want to go to the morgue on Christmas. I have no way of getting there anyway. Would the police give me a ride?

We eventually realize she isn't coming home. "This is all some bullshit!" Eric yells, with hands in the air, and kicks my bedroom door.

"We'll just have Christmas without her. She had to of rented a video," I tell them.

We split up and search the house, but we return to the living room emptyhanded. I flip through the six TV channels about half a dozen times before we all agree to turn it off. Jenny suggests we have hot chocolate. With only two packets and a handful of marshmallows, I make the treat and tell them not to worry about me.

I attempt to get everyone into a festive mood. No one wants to sing carols, but I sing some anyway. Not sure what else to do, I read Bible verses about the birth of Jesus to Jenny. Eric thinks everything is stupid and disappears to his room to play video games. I soon join him, and Jenny watches us battle to death with Chun-Li super kicks and cheater E. Honda hand slaps.

Around midnight, Eric and Jenny are ready for bed, and I go to their rooms to say good night. I hug them, tell them I'm sorry that things can't be better, turn off their lights, and shut their doors. I lay in bed, eyes on my alarm clock, and stubbornly hang on to hope. I think about Eric's grumbled curses about Mother as he turned away from me and covered his head with his blanket. I think about Jenny's sad face as she said thank you. At two thirty, my eyes water, but anger wins. I fall asleep with a heart full of hate.

At six in the morning, my three hours of sleep are interrupted by a loud and full-of-Christmas-cheer Mother, complete with her fake voice and a reek of alcohol. "Merry Christmas!" she yells, barging into my room.

I open my eyes to see her bloodshot eyes, surrounded by smeared makeup. I roll over and cover my head with my pillow. She repeats the rude behavior twice more in Eric's and Jenny's rooms. I listen for my siblings' responses. They are mad as hell and refuse to get out of their beds.

Does she offer an apology or explanation?

Nope.

She asks, "What's wrong with all of y'all? Aren't you excited to open presents early in the morning this year?" She orders us up and gives us five minutes to get to the living room.

Not wanting all hell to break loose, I get up and convince Eric and Jenny to do the same. Mother sits cross-legged on the couch with a big grin on her face. We sit on the floor around the coffee table and open our presents without enthusiasm. We politely say thank you.

Before I can ask about her unopened gifts, she says, "Well, Merry Christmas!" stands, walks to her room, and shuts the door. The three of us stare after her, and then we look at each other. We leave the living room as is and return to our beds. I lie there fuming until I have better things to do like eat breakfast.

We get dressed but miss the Christmas lunch and festivities at a family member's house. The three of us eat last night's leftovers. Mother is unconscious for most of the day.

⁂

Mother follows up her spectacular Christmas performance with a New Year's surprise. "We are moving to Dallas at the end of February."

"What?" the three of us respond simultaneously. We didn't take her seriously when she mentioned the idea right after Vinny left.

She continues, "I want out of Louisiana. I want a better job."

Why did I even expect anything else? Her promises aren't worth a damn. It's miracle she stayed this long. Typical she suddenly wants to leave. God forbid she wait three more months. What the hell am I going to do? I'm so close to graduation. I'm sure as hell not going with her to start over at some new school. I didn't go through all this torturous bullshit just to get up and leave.

I beg her to stay until graduation. Her response leaves me terrified and thrilled. My only options are to find someone to move into our house to take over the payments or find someone to live with. Apparently, it's my responsibility, but if I can somehow make it happen, I'll have three months of freedom, and then I'm off to college.

CHAPTER 32

GROWING

Jon suddenly calls and shows up on my doorstep at the end of January, nine months to the day that he left. At the front door, he hugs and kisses me with the same affection and adoration, but I try not to notice that he feels unnervingly strange and unfamiliar to me. We haven't spoken since he left, and we exchanged all of one letter back in May.

On the couch in my room, I crawl into his lap, and we hold each other. "Your hair has gotten so long," he comments while twirling the end of a lock between his fingers, "but you're still short."

"Hey!" I say and elbow him in the ribs. He pulls my hair in return and turns my face toward his. When the long, slow kiss ends, he stares at my face like he's trying to simultaneously memorize and reacquaint himself with my features. I do the same to him. When I raise my eyebrows, he says, "I've missed you. How have you been? How's school?"

"This year has been crazy," I say and move to sit beside him. I explain that I'm co-captain of the color guard, and I tell him about losing a shoe during a band competition on the muddy football field at Northwestern University. I describe the school clubs and how I write for the school newspaper. My mouth runs halfway through the homecoming dance and stops abruptly after Jon says, "Daniel."

My eyes flick to his, and I see smothered disappointment. "I, uh, we…" I grasp for words that won't hurt him.

"You turned seventeen, and I wasn't here."

Loneliness had become another burden to carry. Daniel fit my type exactly, but he was a wisp of shadow compared to Jonathan. There was no replacing him. After homecoming, I reverted back to stone, and Daniel fell off my radar and into obscurity. Beyond the dating restrictions, Andrew couldn't understand why I wouldn't give anyone else a chance. His persistence finally wore me down. I told him about my long-distance relationship and confessed that I had doubts.

Shortly after, a football player named Ryan pursued me. All his friends seemed to be in on the chase. Once I put aside the guilt and said yes, Ryan got Mother's permission, took me out on dates, drove me home after school, and waved at me when he went out onto the field. The first time I went to his house was for a Christmas party with his friends. I met his parents and siblings, who were so excited to finally meet me and showered me with gifts. Even Mother was on her best behavior whenever he came over to the house.

A normal life was not in my cards. The fear of others knowing the truth about Mother left me no choice but to shut people out and hurt them. A few weeks after Christmas, I broke up with Ryan and burned all the connections I had to newfound friends.

I explain none of this and decide to keep things simple. "Jon, I'm sorry. Despite my best efforts not to notice other guys and ignore the guys interested in me, things happened." I tell him about the guys giving me attention along with their phone numbers. I summarize the handful of dates I went on with different people. All the while, he watches our combined hands, and I see the jealousy on his face despite his words of understanding. When I tell him that I had one short-lived relationship with a football player, he tenses and doesn't move.

"Jon," I say, but he remains stoic and continues to stare toward the windows. I try to find the right words to comfort and reassure him, but then his eyes meet mine and he quietly asks, "Did you sleep with him?"

Not expecting the question, because my mind didn't even go there, I don't say anything right away. Looking away from me, he whispers, "I won't be able to stand it if you were with him. If he touched you like that."

I jostle and pull his hand, but he won't look at me, so I wait patiently until he does. "Now, you know me better than that, Jonathan. I deserve a little more credit. We only kissed."

"I just wanted to make sure. I know how guys are, and, well, you're beautiful and affectionate and…" he doesn't finish his thought but instead puts his free hand to my cheek and says, "I want to be your first, if you still love me."

My cheeks burn. "Yes. I'm still yours," I say and crawl back onto his lap to kiss him.

Eric and Jenny interrupt with a knock on the door. They come in for a second to say hello. Jon looks around and asks me, "Where's your Mom?"

"Oh, who knows? She's hardly ever home these days."

"And she's cool with me being here?"

"She doesn't have a choice. I'm seventeen, and she's not here. Not my fault. Plus, you already have permission, remember? We just had to wait for my birthday."

"Oh, yeah, that's right," he says with a smile before changing to a more serious tone. "Is she treating you any better?"

"No, it's about the same as before."

"Tina, you promised me you would get help if anything happened."

"She hasn't hit me since right after you left, but she still treats me like shit. Just more yelling, screaming, calling me horrible names. I'm stuck here being a slave. There are times I can't take it anymore, but then she disappears for days."

I see the lecture he's about to give me, so I remind him before he can start, "She's not all bad. It comes and goes. Sometimes she nice, and sometimes she's a raging bitch. That's how she's always been." He doesn't say anything, so I continue, "She's moving to Dallas, anyway, at the end of next month. I've got to find a place to live so I can finish the school year."

"What? How could she do that to you? Not that I'm surprised. Why can't she just wait?"

"Your guess is as good as mine," I say, rubbing my forehead.

Silence surrounds us as he gets lost in thought.

"What's up? What are you thinking?" I ask. He answers with a refusal to leave me. He wants me to pack my stuff and move across the country to live with him. He says I can go to college there.

"And how would that work, exactly? Your underage girlfriend living on a military base. It's impossible," I say with a huff.

"Once you turn eighteen, you would be my wife—that's if you still want to be with me," he says. As I process the word *wife*, I barely hear him continue, "Do you understand what I'm asking?"

When I find my voice, I respond, "Jon, that's not funny."

"I'm being serious."

"No, you're being ridiculous. Besides, you don't even have a ring."

"I was going to wait until after you graduated, but..." He reaches over to his jacket lying across the arm of the couch and pulls something out of a pocket. Eyes wide, I look at it and then at him. I slowly take the small box and hold it between my hands, the weight so light and yet so heavy.

"Tina? Say something."

I hear him, but I'm too busy thinking—always automatically analyzing, always weighing the cons and seeing how difficult they will be.

"Tina. Please. What are you thinking?"

I finally say, "You'll always be gone, leaving me alone in an unfamiliar place with unfamiliar people. I'll have no family until you come back."

"Yes, it will be difficult at first, but we will be together, finally together. We won't have limitations or rules. No more waiting. We'll have the rest of our lives together."

I think about his words and the possibilities of that life. I think about how Mother met my twenty-three-year-old father at

England Air Force Base. She married him at the age of fifteen, partially due to my grandmother abandoning her in a somewhat similar fashion. Three years later, I came along and then Eric when I was two, followed by Jenny when I was five.

"And do you expect us to have children?" I ask.

"Well, eventually, I hope. Whenever you're ready, depending on what you want to do about college—or never, if that's what you want too."

"What if you're gone for another nine months or a year? And wouldn't we constantly move? What if you're injured or killed?" I ask him.

"Tina, I can't control those things. This is my life. I love you, and I want you to be with me. That's all I can offer."

Before I can respond, he says, with regret in his voice, "I always knew it was a possibility this could happen. That you'd grow up while I was away and change your mind. Everything is happening so fast now. I come back, and you've changed."

How to respond? I do love him, but he's right. Things are changing—have changed. I barely considered what exactly would happen with us after graduation. Always an impossible dream, like a mirage, and now that I'm reaching my destination, I'm not so sure anymore. I mean, we don't know each other enough to be married. His long absences left room for other dreams.

"Jon, I love you, but you're right. I've changed in the time you've been gone. I'm not sure what I want anymore. I'm sorry."

"Tina, you don't have to make up your mind right this second. Just think about it, and make your decision after graduation. I'll be back in a few months. We can talk about it then."

I hand him back the unopened box and tell him to keep it until then.

CHAPTER 33

SEPARATED

My grandmother drives away with Jenny at the beginning of February, which leaves only two of us for Mother to rant and rave at with her vicious commentary and expectations. Eric and I care less and are one step below open rebellion. I try to keep my mouth shut and uphold the peace until moving day, but Mommy Dearest tries to fight Eric, and he gives her a taste of her own medicine. *Ha!* Unfortunately for me, one week later, he's on a plane to Chicago. I'm left alone to pack for the move.

My cousin Stella and her new husband decide not to move in with me, which leaves my situation precarious. I only have three weeks to find somewhere to go. Mother refuses to stay one moment longer. When I ask her what I'm supposed to do, she tells me, "Not my problem."

Two weeks before she leaves, Mother says that I can live with Aunt Evelyn. Then, one week until the move, Evelyn decides she's going to England on a trial separation from her husband for a month or so. I'm shit out of luck until Sharron, another family friend, offers to take me in, and Mother agrees to pay her two hundred dollars a month for room and board.

A few months prior, I'd had a severe sinus infection. Mother came home after getting her car washed and her nails done, without the medicine I requested. When I'd asked her about it, she told me, "Oh, well," and refused to go back out.

Sharron is the most responsible adult I know who lives close, so I walked about two miles to her house on the other side of Louisiana College and asked if she had any cold medicine. Sharron took me to the store, got me a bag full of every medicine possible, and drove me home. Mother didn't say a word as Sharron chewed her out right in front of me.

Sharron tells me I won't have to do housework or cook. Her only requirement is for me to watch her two kids on the weekends when she wants to go out. I trust her and agree to her terms.

Luckily, Jon calls an hour before the house phone is disconnected. I give him Sharron's address and phone number so he'll be able to find me when he comes back at the end of March.

The next day, I'm torn between feeling the absolute joy of being rid of Mother and the absolute sorrow of leaving the only place I called home for a significant amount of time. Everything in the house is loaded into a giant moving van, minus my meager belongings.

Mother drops me off at Sharron's house. Out on the driveway, I unload my suitcase and three small boxes. Mother hands Sharron two hundred dollars, gives me a quick hug, tells me "good luck," and leaves. As she drives away, Sharron looks at me with a shake of her head and says, "Wow. What a bitch. You leave your kid, and that's it. Well, at least you don't have to deal with her anymore."

I become an addition to Sharron's little family unit, but I feel strange with routine, peace, and free time. Undisturbed, I do homework and research colleges using a book from the local library. Sharron's five-year-old son is adorable, and we play together all the time. I'm grateful for the room I share with her daughter, but I miss my room and privacy. I miss going over to Andrew's house in the mornings before school. I miss my dog, Sasha.

She can't be at Sharron's house because the landlord doesn't allow dogs, which leaves the poor girl at the Magnolia Street house. The back door stays open, so she can go in and out. Every day, rain or shine, I walk there after Sharron gets home from work. Sometimes I speed walk straight there after school so I can get to Sharron's house before her son comes home from daycare.

Sasha waits for me by the fence and jumps up and down when she sees me. We play ball, I brush out her thick white-and-brown coat, and I refill her buckets of food and water.

Before I leave, I stare at my small stack of boxes and the empty fish tank sitting alone in the corner of my room. I think about the good times when my family was together. Sometimes I sit on the floor with my back up against the wall, where my couch used to be, and sing random snippets of sad songs. Sasha puts her head in my lap, and we listen to my voice echo through the empty house. I try not to cry every time I leave her.

CHAPTER 34

COLLEGE

From my large list of colleges, I select only four, because I can afford their application fees. I withdraw the last of my old job money and close my bank account. Some of the cash goes to postage and the rest to Sharron, who writes four checks. As I stare at the empty essay portions of the applications, I think about how I wanted to be a writer when I was little, and I rub my forehead.

⋏

My guidance counselor, with her beehive blond hair, is a mean old crone. Her eye-rolling and condescending tone of voice piss me off as she proceeds to tell me that I'll never get into college if I apply to only four—my grades aren't good enough, and neither is my ACT score. She hands me a bunch of scholarship applications and says "good luck" before telling me to go back to class.

When I get home, I sift through the stack of papers and find only one that I qualify for. I write an essay explaining why I want to be a marine biologist and mail it off with a mediocre hope it will arrive by the deadline.

Weeks later, when I drop off homework for an absent student with the school secretary, I'm practically accosted with niceness from the old beehive. She graciously invites me into her office, where I learn I'm one of three finalists for the scholarship. I'm dumbfounded, mostly by her change in demeanor. She informs me that I'm to report for an interview with a panel of three judges, and she instructs me to wear something nice, preferably a dress. As I leave, she pats me on the back and says, "See, I knew you could do it."

I start to panic on my way back to class.

Me? Talk to strangers? About what? What do I know that they would want to know? Am I to tell them about my life? How well I can clean a house, that I can't cook, and I hate my mother? Jesus, I'm sweating already. Lord, help me. I purposely don't talk to classmates I don't know to avoid talking and awkwardness, and now I'm supposed to talk to complete strangers about some random topic. Shit!

▲

I'm in full-on panic attack mode. Jackie tries to calm me down before I exit the car, but no amount of encouragement can stop my shaking hands. I look in the visor mirror and see that the humidity has done a number on my hair.

I enter the building and wait in a hallway next to two seniors from other schools, one with a tie and the other in a simple black dress. Here I sit in the nicest thing I own, the puffy black and flower-print dress I wore to Jackie's wedding last year. My competitors look professional, and I feel like a clown.

Of course, I'm last, which gives me plenty of time to stew in my anxiety and go to the restroom ten times. Upon entering the interview room, I sit in a metal folding chair in front of three people behind a white table. I feel like I'm on trial for a murder I didn't commit.

They ask me to explain the importance of voting, or something to that effect. I know the answer, but the question is unexpected, and I need time to formulate a response.

I can't control the anxiety as it works its way up from the pit of my stomach and into my throat, where it disconnects my mouth from my brain, leaving my skull to silently vibrate as the anxiety invades and throws all coherent thought into chaos.

I've never voted before. How the hell am I supposed to truly know the significance beyond what I read in a textbook last year in civics class? I've never cared nor had to care about politics or voting or jury duty for that matter. I'm just a poor, homeless idiot. This is a disaster. I hope the winner uses the money wisely.

My face burns with the realization that they have been staring at me for a while. I sputter out some nonsense and swallow a giant gulp of embarrassment.

The female judge says, "My dear, are you okay?" to which I reply, "Not really."

Another one asks, "Is that all you have to say about the topic?"

I reply, "Yes, sir."

The last one shakes his head and says I can go, and I do, straight to the car where I tell Jackie what happened and try not to die from the shame.

"You had it. All you had to do was answer a simple question," she sighs with a sour face on Monday after she had me paged to come down to her office. Old Queen Bee is back to her usual unpleasant self. She mumbles under her breath about disappointment and how it would have been good for the school.

CHAPTER 35

EMPTY

I pick at my fingernails and break one and then another. I leave the living room window and force myself to sit down on the couch. My right foot shakes as I think.

Jon's right. I changed in tiny increments after each goodbye, and upon each return, he's more and more of a stranger. Do I actually know him anymore? Can I still trust him? His love for me may not have changed, but his life has since that summer long ago, and I'm not sure I can fit into it and be truly happy. I'm at a crossroad. Which direction? I can't see how he'll fit into my life, which will soon begin. Maybe I'll think differently when I see him and we're alone.

Jon is right on time for our first official date. When I open the door, I find him grinning behind a bouquet of flowers. He gives me a quick hug and then looks me up and down and says, "You look so pretty. I've never seen you in a dress."

I introduce him to Sharron, who puts the flowers in a vase for me. He thanks her for allowing us to go out on a school night and says he'll have me home by ten. Before we walk out the door, she pulls me aside and tells him that I'll be out in a minute.

Through the kitchen window I see him by the passenger door of his car.

She says, "Ooh, girl, he is handsome. Now I understand all the talk of Jon this and Jon that. Just remember you have school tomorrow."

I scrunch my face at her, and she says, "Y'all have all day Saturday. You can come home whenever you want then. You're practically a grown woman. Have some fun for once in your life."

"Really?" I say, surprised.

"I was young once too. You're a good kid, Tina. You deserve it. Just don't tell your mother anything about it. No one wants to deal with that."

I laugh and say, "Thanks, Sharron, and thanks for loaning me the dress and for the make-up." I give her a hug before she shuts the door behind me.

⁂

I fail to ignore the panic building in my chest. As Jon drives, I look at his hand in mine and then at his profile.

I want a stable life and someone who belongs only to me. I'm too young to be a wife. I haven't even done anything yet. I can't move to an army base, and I can't marry him. I have to end this. What am I going to do? I have no idea how to do this. I can't break up with him at a restaurant. I can't go all evening pretending everything is fine and then break up with him at the end. But I love him, and we've waited for each other. This day has been a long time coming. Maybe if I...

With the need to prove something, combined with the complete madness of waiting so long to be with him, we drive all of six blocks, and I tell him to pull over, which he does.

To his surprise, I take off our seatbelts. He gets out half a "what?" before I grab and kiss him. He chuckles as he kisses me back, until I maneuver into his lap. Between each of my feverish kisses, he says, "Whoa. Okay. Tina. Wait." He looks around, despite my attempts to keep him occupied. A long line of bright headlights passes by us.

"There's too much traffic here," he tells me and stops my advances with a gentle push on my upper arms. I barely hear him say, "Let me move us somewhere less…exposed."

I shift back to my seat but leave my seatbelt unbuckled. I stare out the side window and feel the car move forward. *It's no use. There's nothing there anymore. Just emptiness. I'm sure the sex would be great, but there's no feeling, no longing, no great expansive love I once felt for this man. There's nothing left.*

He drives a few more blocks and turns onto a more secluded street. This time he pulls me to him, and we resume where we left off. His mouth is gentle at first, but I kiss him like my life depends on it, my last attempt to feel something, anything. He responds in kind, and I feel him harden beneath me. Our hands explore anywhere and everywhere, but the effort is useless. The future I once hoped for is now a void, and there's no escape. I suddenly hear Mother's voice inside my head.

Push him away like everyone else. He broke your heart first. Time to return the favor. You'll be the one leaving this time. Better to end it and stop stringing him along, you tease. Let him find someone who deserves his love. You can't trust him anyway. You can't trust anyone. He only wants to fuck you, and off he'll go. How can he love someone like you? No one will ever love you like you want. You couldn't even make your own parents love you properly.

I abruptly stop. He goes still as well and asks, "What's wrong?"

"I can't," I tell him and crawl back into the passenger seat. Facing away from him, I hide my watering eyes as despair and self-hatred cloud my thoughts. I apologize for my rash behavior, but he kisses me and tries to pull me back, to hold me, and to put my hands back on his body. I tell him no, and he releases me.

"Tina, why are you acting so crazy?"

"Crazy? Crazy is our relationship. Letting it drag on and on. Why do you keep coming back here? You have the whole world and adventures, and you show up here expecting me to wait for you. For years. Well, I can't do it anymore." *Nothing is coming out of my mouth right.*

"Tina, stop. You don't mean that," he says and tries to take my hand, but I jerk away.

"No, Jon. We are done. You just want to get laid, and I'm not giving you what you want. I'm waiting to get married…"

…to someone who I love completely. Someone who is free and not in the military. Never again will I fall for a soldier! Never again will I be homeless!

"But, Tina, I want to…"

"No. I'm not moving in with you, and I'm not marrying you. I have a life of my own, and I'm leaving. We are over. I don't want to see you anymore. Please take me back."

The confusion and shock on his face becomes anger, and he says, "Fine."

We sit in silence as he drives. *After everything we've been through, I can't leave things like this. I don't want to hurt him more than necessary. I don't want him to hate me. I want him to understand. I have to fix this.*

I have six blocks left to rearrange everything that I want to say to him. When he stops in front of Sharron's house, I begin with, "I'm sorry…"

"Whatever," he interrupts.

"Jon, please, I—"

"Just go!" he yells, without looking at me.

I get out, and as soon as I close the door, he speeds off. I stand in the middle of the dark street and watch until his taillights disappear in the distance. *He left me. Just like that.* A car's headlights stop behind me. I hear honking but remain motionless until the driver yells, "Crazy girl, get out of the road!"

Dazed, I enter the house. Sharron meets me in the kitchen and says, "What happened? You've been gone for less than thirty minutes."

My face crumples at the sight of the flowers, and I tell her that I broke up with him. She hugs me and guides me to the couch. "But why?" she asks and hands me some tissue as we sit. "You left, and everything was all right. You have plans on Saturday."

"I kissed him, and there was nothing. I don't love him anymore. I hurt him, and I feel so guilty. I tried to explain, but it came out all wrong, and he got angry and refused to listen to anything else. Then he drove off."

"Oh, honey. I'm sorry. You haven't even gone on a proper date with him. Can't you salvage things? Maybe if you spend some time together on Saturday, you can get to know him again."

"There's no point. He's leaving. I'm leaving. Our lives will be so different. I'm never falling for anyone in the military ever again! It's too painful. I feel like my chest is caving in."

"Honey, sounds to me like you still love him, and you're just being practical," she says, rubbing my shoulder. "And don't say never. There's lots of handsome men in uniform and one may catch your eye someday."

"Not after this," I tell her and shake my head.

"Go wash your face. I'll warm you up some gumbo, and there's chocolate cake for dessert."

"Thanks, Sharron. You're a good mom."

⊥

Jon calls on Saturday and Sunday, but I refuse to talk to him, despite Sharron's encouragement. She repeats my words to him each time, "Jonathan, she's not going to talk to you. It's over. Please don't call back."

I hate him. Have to. He yelled at me. He left me in the street. Alone. In the dark.

CHAPTER 36

MONEY

Graduation looms closer, and I find myself with too many things to pay for and no money. I didn't realize being a senior is so expensive—ring, cap, gown, graduation invitations, stamps, pictures, yearbook, and prom. Nor did I anticipate a lack of parental funds for basics like dog food and toiletries. Sharron is already fighting with Mother for the next two hundred dollars.

A few weeks after Jonathan and I ended, Jackie comes to my rescue and gets me a job back at the restaurant where I worked before. Our shifts of Friday and Saturday nights and Sunday mornings match, so she drives me. For the most part, I stay with her on the weekends unless Sharron needs me to babysit.

I can't keep walking back and forth to Sasha, and there's no one to check on her on the weekends while I'm at work. Sharron convinces her landlord to allow Sasha to stay, and he charges a seventy-five-dollar fee to keep her outside.

Since there's no fence, I tie her to the wooden doghouse in the backyard, which works for about ten minutes after everyone goes to bed. Sasha howls nonstop until I bring her into the house.

She sleeps next to me on the floor, and every morning I tie her back up before I leave for school. The Magnolia Street house gets broken into. My boxes are rummaged through, and my fish tank is stolen.

Eventually, Sharron gets pissed that I'm not there to watch her kids on the weekends, and she gives me an ultimatum. "Stay home as per our original agreement, or find somewhere else to live." I try to reason with her and explain my money problems, but she's adamant.

I have no choice but to pack my belongings and go. Jackie lives too far away, and with her work schedule, I have no way to get back and forth to school.

Jackie comes to the rescue again and finds Evelyn, who will be home from England in a week. I tell Sharron that I'll move to Evelyn's house like I was supposed to do in the first place, and she gets angry. When Jackie and Evelyn help me move out, I try to thank Sharron for taking me in before I leave. I don't understand why, but she won't speak to me.

⋏

I change my address and settle into Evelyn's daughter's old room. My few boxes huddle together in another corner. My uncle and aunt, Mother's brother and his wife, take turns transporting me back and forth to school. Jackie picks me up on Friday afternoons for work, and I stay with her on the weekends. Sasha happily has free reign over Evelyn's large, fenced backyard.

During the week, I'm left to my own devices. Evelyn and her husband work late, but she always has dinner prepared in containers for me to warm up, complete with instructions, alternate food selections, and often her location and estimated time of arrival. I look forward to her little notes taped to the fridge, microwave, or stove. When Evelyn and her husband are home, they frequently argue, and despite their efforts to work it out, I'm doubtful they will.

After school one day, I find a stack of mail addressed to me on the counter, some of which are graduation invitations from friends at both high schools. I still haven't sent mine out, so, sitting on the floor next to my bed, I dig through a box for my address book. I come across the stack of letters from Jon, and at that moment, Evelyn walks through the open bedroom door and hands me a roll of stamps.

"You didn't have to do that. Here," I say, reaching for my purse next to me. "How much do I owe you?"

"Save your money for prom. I made the salon appointment for two o'clock like you wanted."

"Thanks, Evelyn," I say and look down at the stack of letters in my lap.

"What are those?" she asks.

"They're from Jonathan. I suppose I should throw them out."

"No, don't do that. One day, when you're much older, you'll be glad you kept them," she says and walks out of the room.

I pick at the edge of the top envelope, run a finger over his name, and put them back in the box.

CHAPTER 37
BESTIES

The University of Miami sends me an acceptance letter, but that's not happening at twenty-five grand per semester. Andrew and I decide Nicholls State University is the place to be. They have a great marine biology program and, more importantly, I can afford the tuition. All I need to do is submit the rest of my financial aid paperwork. Jackie drives me to Thibodaux for the campus tour, but we arrive too late. We can't find Andrew anywhere and have no way to contact him.

When I see him at lunch on Monday, he says, "So, let me guess, Monkey Butt, you showed up two hours late and missed the tour."

"How did you know, Smelly Cheese?" I ask with a grin, which earns me an eye roll.

We grab trays, slide down the buffet line for taco boats, and sit down. He tells me about everything I missed on the tour and then asks, "Hey, you busy on Friday?"

"Maybe. Depends on what harebrained idea you got cooking in that thick skull of yours."

"Remember when we went fishing a while back with your brother at Buhlow Lake and how we talked about camping?"

"Yeah," I laugh. "That was the day you fell in."

"That was so not funny," he says, smacking me on the arm. "I was soaking wet."

"Oh, yes it was," I say, laughing even louder, and put my hand over my mouth when a teacher gives me a funny look.

"Alright. Laugh it up," he says, with a folding of arms. I wipe my eyes as I snicker, and he adds, "You finished?"

"Yes, yes. What about camping?" I reply and continue to eat.

"Let's do it. Julie's in. We can get a group together. Get some tents." He drops his voice to a whisper, "I can get hold of some alcohol again."

"At Buhlow? Is camping even allowed there?" I ask and think of all the possible crazy shenanigans we could get into.

"I think so. I don't see why not. I've seen people camping there."

"Okay. I'm in."

"Just don't try swimming in the lake, and no howling at the moon."

"And what's wrong with howling at the moon? And besides, it's a lake, not a swamp this time, and it's not January."

"You were so wasted," he chuckles.

"And whose fault was that?"

"I didn't make you drink all those strawberry daiquiris."

"Yeah, but you kept making them until the blender died, and then all of a sudden, here Tina, try some Boone's Farm," I say, mimicking his voice.

"It took me the whole day to clean up the red mess from the daiquiris you and Julie threw everywhere. My uncle would have killed me. We pretty much destroyed his cabin."

"Hey! You started that war. We just finished it," I say with a smirk.

"That was an awesome New Year's Eve," he says, laughing.

"Totally. Hey, I have to go to my locker before the bell rings. Let me know the details. I just have to make sure my Aunt Evelyn's cool with it."

"Will she let you?"

"Oh, yeah. She pretty lenient about everything."

⋏

At dusk, multiple tents populate a small clearing at the end of a road. A roaring fire and blaring music hold back the otherwise quiet dark of the forest. Everyone drank up most of the alcohol, except for Andrew and his girlfriend, Julie, who left twenty-five minutes ago in his Dad's pickup truck. They should be back any minute with more food.

I dance and sing around the flickering flames, with a red Solo cup in my hand. The rest of the group laughs at my antics, and I try to persuade them to join me. My friend Seth caves.

"Tina, I've never seen you so…you're different when you're at school," he says, half dancing, half walking around with me.

"Well, that's because you—or anyone else, for that matter—doesn't really know me," I tell him and spin around without spilling my drink.

"I can see why Andrew likes to hang out with you. You're fun."

"Well thanks there, sweetheart," I say, imitating Humphrey Bogart, and dance away into the dark. I stop between two trees at the edge of the lake. My eyes are drawn to the smiling Cheshire Cat moon in the dark water below me. I howl at my friend rising over the other side and listen to the quick echo disappear. I think of Jon and imagine him in some faraway place, looking up at the moon at the same time. Seth grabs me before I fall in.

"You're my hero," I say like a damsel.

"That was close. Andrew would have killed me if you ended up in the lake. I'm in charge of you until he gets back."

My hero guides me back to the bonfire and then tries to be slick and attempts to lure me into one of the tents for some alone time.

"My dear Seth, I may be drunk, but I'm not a slut, you naughty boy," I say loudly as I step out of the tent. Everyone laughs. Seth exits with an innocent smile and a shrug and returns to his seat with the rest of the group.

"Andy would have kicked my ass anyway," he says to them.

"And afterwards, your ass would have been thrown in the lake," someone comments with a laugh.

I don't get to make my comment, because three cop cars roll up with flashing red and blue lights. I instantly sober up and toss my Solo into the bushes. *Oh, shit! We are so busted! Where is Andrew? Goddammit! My mother is going to kill me! Evelyn's never going to let me out of her sight ever again!*

With flashlights in hand, the cops search around like they already know what we've been up to. They say fires here are illegal and some other nonsense before the interrogations begin. I give the female officer my name, age, and Evelyn's name and phone number, but I refuse to answer any more questions. She retrieves my Solo cup and asks if it is mine. I tell her maybe.

"Can I have it?" I ask, to which she asks, "Why?"

"So I can put out the fire."

I spend the next five minutes dousing the flames with lake water. I get soot all over my shoes from moving the logs around. Andrew pulls up as I finish.

All eight of us, along with the tents, backpacks, and ice chests, pile up in the back of the pickup truck, and we are escorted to the police station. Andrew warns us not to say a word.

No one is arrested, but our guardians are called at one o'clock in the morning. In solidarity, we remain silent when the officers question us. We sit on the damn prisoner bench and get lectured about the hazards of underage drinking until we slowly disappear a few at a time.

⁂

Evelyn shows up, and we get in the car.

"Are you hurt?"

"No, ma'am."

"Are you drunk?"

"I was until the police showed up."

"Yeah, that will sober you up real quick."

"Anything else?" I ask, expecting the worse.

"Nope. We're good."

I face the passenger side window and wait for her to change her mind at any moment. Once home, I go directly outside to visit with Sasha before bed. I lean up against the covered porch post and toss the ball out into the backyard. Sasha drops the ball in front of me, but I neglect to pick it up or respond to her whimper as my eyes focus on the darkness before us. The glass back door slides open. I glance over my shoulder to see Evelyn exit with a lit cigarette.

"You okay?" she asks. "Feeling sick?"

"No, just scared."

"Of the police?"

"No. About what is going to happen when you tell Mother."

She looks at me as she inhales and blows the smoke away from us. "I wasn't planning on telling her."

"What?" I say and burst into tears.

She hugs me. "Tina. It's no big deal. This doesn't even scratch the surface of the mountain of shit your mother and I pulled when we were much younger than you."

"I'm sorry I didn't tell you about the alcohol."

"Hey. I'm surprised it took you this long to get into some trouble. Just give me a heads-up next time if there's a possibility I may need to get you from the police station again. I'll be more prepared—like dressed and ready to go."

As I laugh, she wipes my face with her hand. "You of all people deserve a little fun and trouble," she says and walks back to the door.

"Aunt Evelyn?" I call after her, and she stops before going in. "Are you seriously not going to tell Mom?"

"She's my best friend, and we have no secrets, but on this particular item, I swear. It will be our little secret. Now get to bed. You have to work tomorrow."

CHAPTER 38

STAG

Aside from a few adventures with my best friend, I concentrate strictly on school, work, and surviving to the end. My grades are going up, but my social life is nonexistent. I work every weekend, and since I moved to Evelyn's house, I can't make phone calls. We live in another area code, which means long-distance calls to my friends are charged more per minute.

Then there's the fact that ever since I broke up with Ryan back in January, I've been excommunicated from most social circles. Apparently, I'm off-limits, too—at least that's Andrew's theory as to why not one single person asks me to prom. Or maybe I have simply walled myself off from most everyone and became a quiet loner once again. Moving constantly has taught me not to hold on to people. I don't plan on sticking around after graduation, especially if I get to visit Chicago for the summer.

Doesn't help that the lunch schedules change, and I'm the only one of my group with the pleasure of second lunch. I enter the cafeteria with hope, but since everyone is so cliquey, I have an entire table to myself. The second day, Sharron's daughter invites me to sit with her and other freshmen, which I'm grateful for until I see my classmates snickering. *To hell with that.* I spend the last month of school outside, alone in the senior area. I sit on a bench in the sun, stare at the parking lot, and eat a lunch of Snickers and Dr. Pepper.

Before I know it, prom is upon us. Andrew, Julie, and I go shopping for outfits. I can't afford to buy a dress, so they accompany me to a rental place. The fruitless search ends when Andrew hands me a long, tight-fitting, sleeveless, green velvet gown with a rhinestone front and collar. Figures he found the one. I purchase matching shoes and sparkly, fake diamond earrings. My long mop of hair will be in an updo. Jackie says she'll loan me her makeup.

For the entire last week before prom, Andrew and Julie try to convince me to ride with them.

"Why won't you just ride with us?" Andrew whispers during our math class.

"I'm fine. Jackie will drive me. No big deal," I whisper back.

"Tina, you're not showing up alone," he insists.

"I don't mind. It's no big deal. Alone is kinda my thing these days."

The bell suddenly rings, and we gather our belongings. Andrew refuses to give up and continues, "Absolutely not! And I'm not taking no for an answer this time. I'll throw you over my shoulder and put you in the car myself."

"Fine, Andrew. I don't want you messing up my hair," I say with a laugh and an eye roll, because I know he would do it.

Jackie and I work the Friday before prom, which happens to be my last day. After the restaurant closes for the night, everyone rushes to clean and set up for the tomorrow. As they begin to leave, my coworkers stop at my station, hand me extra wads of cash from their tips, wish me well, and say goodbye.

One of the waiters, whom I joke around with all the time, asks me about tomorrow. "So, who's the lucky guy?"

"Ethan, I don't have a date," I say, laughing at his question.

"How is that even possible?" he asks.

Other coworkers hear our conversation and start questioning me as well.

"I don't know," I say with a shrug and try not to care or blush. I wave them away from me, turn my back to the group, and continue my duties. Everyone disappears except Ethan. Out of the corner of my eye, I see him still next to me.

"Tina," he says, gently taking my elbow, and turns me toward him.

He lets go when I look up at him and say, "Yes, Ethan?"

He goes to say something else but stops. I follow his line of sight to the bar and see his girlfriend, Valerie, putting away bottles of liquor. "I'll be right back. Stay here," he says.

"Should I wait in this exact spot?" I tease.

"No," he laughs. "I mean don't leave, yet, with Jackie."

I give him a salute and say, "Sir, yes, sir."

He laughs, again, and walks to the bar with a determined look on his face.

Fifteen minutes later, Jackie and I are about to leave when Ethan and Valerie approach. Valerie has a big grin on her face and starts the conversation, "Tina, Ethan and I talked it over, and if it is okay with you, and if we can arrange things with Jackie…"

Ethan interrupts, "I'd like to take you to prom."

"What? Seriously? No. Y'all are sweet, but you don't have to do that."

"We insist," Valerie says as she takes my arm and leads me away. I can't hear the details, but Ethan explains things to Jackie. Valerie continues, "Don't you think Ethan's handsome?"

"Um…yes, he is…" I tell her truthfully.

"Good. So that's not a problem."

"Okay," I say, not knowing how else to respond.

"He's a perfect gentleman too."

"I'm sure he is, but how is he going to find a—"

"He owns a tux. So, we're set?"

"You're not going to let me refuse, are you?"

"Nope. Come on. He's a good dancer."

I laugh. "How can I say no?"

"Yes! Awesome! This is going to be so fun! You'll see. He'll even take pictures and everything."

"Thank you, Valerie," I say and she gives me a big hug.

"Thank Ethan. This was all his idea." She leads me back to the rest of our group.

Ethan gives us a wink and asks, "Are we all set?"

"Yes, I accept your offer," I say and crack up when Ethan grabs us for a group hug.

On our way home, Jackie fills me in on all the arrangements until she turns left into a bar parking lot.

"Jackie, what are we doing?"

"Celebrating your graduation," she says, with a mischievous grin.

We enter the smoky bar, and there are a bunch of our coworkers and Jackie's friends. I sit at a table with them near the live band, and Jackie gets drinks from her bartender friend. She quickly returns and hands me a giant foam cup with a straw.

"What the hell is this?" I ask her and take the cup.

"Water," she says loudly and sits down. She leans toward my face. "Crown and Coke. Drink it," she orders in a whisper and gives me a wink.

"Yes, ma'am."

⋏

I'm plastered. All the way to Jackie's house, I loudly sing along to her Ozzie Osborne cassette tape until we turn into the driveway. My voice fades as memories of Jon end my drunken joy.

Jackie asks, "You okay?"

"I loved him, Jackie."

"I know, baby. I know you did," she says.

When the car stops moving, I keep moving and immediately feel queasy. I didn't know the rules. No one has ever warned me about drinking on an empty stomach. I spend the next hour puking up my guts and wake up around noon, hungover. With two hours left until my hair appointment, I lie on the love seat with a cool rag on my head and try to keep up with Hercules and Xena as they run around on TV kicking ass. I hope the Advil, crackers, and coffee entering my face will help.

With permission from Jackie, I make a long-distance phone call. I tell Andrew that I got a last-minute date, and I'll meet him at the restaurant. He doesn't sound too thrilled about the change in plan.

"Andrew, are you okay? You sound upset."

"No, everything is fine."

"What's wrong?" I ask.

"Nothing," he responds.

"Look, I don't have time for this. I'm going to be late for my hair appointment, and I'm hungover."

"What?"

"Oh, don't shout," I say, trying to control the painful vibration between my ears. "I'll explain when I see you."

"Fine," he says and hangs up.

CHAPTER 39

PROM

Ethan knocks on the door five minutes early, and I open it.
"Wow! You look amazing! You clean up well, kid," he tells me.

"Thanks. You don't look too bad yourself, for an old guy," I tease. He's a knockout in the tux.

"Hey, I'm only twenty three. That would make Jackie ancient."

"Hey, I heard that," Jackie says, on her way down the stairs.

After he puts a corsage on my left wrist, I say, "Ethan, thank you. You didn't have to do that."

"Do you honestly think Valerie would have let me leave the house without one? I don't know who's having more fun with this," he says with a laugh.

As we leave, he tells Jackie, "I'll have Cinderella here home by midnight."

"You kids have too much fun," she calls after us.

⋏

We meet Andrew and Julie at Tunk's Cypress Inn on Kincaid Lake. Many of our classmates are here, and I ignore the stares. Andrew is curt with Ethan from the moment we see him in the parking lot, which progresses to downright rudeness during dinner. I give Ethan another apologetic look and silently mouth "I'm so sorry." He shrugs his shoulder, shakes his head, and mouths back, "It's okay."

Andrew's next snarky comment has me on my feet, and I insist he helps me find the restroom. He follows me straight to the restroom hallway, where I let him have it. "What the hell is your problem?"

"Tina, who is this guy? Man? Person? He's way too old for you."

"Like we explained, Andrew, we worked together. He has a girlfriend, for Christ's sake! He's just doing me a favor so I wouldn't go to prom by myself."

"You were supposed to go with me and Julie."

"Well, plans changed. I'm sorry. You would rather me go alone? Really, Andrew? I thought you of all people would be happy for me."

"Yeah, well, everyone's going to think…"

"Think what? First of all, I don't give a rat's ass about what everyone thinks. They don't know me, and they don't know what my life has been like, especially these past four months."

"And how has that been? I don't see you, you don't call me, and you show up with this guy and—"

"Andrew, I'm not discussing my 'oh so fabulous' life right now. I've got a lot of shit going on, and I don't need this. You're supposed to be my best friend, so start acting like it, and quit being an asshole to Ethan!"

"Fine," he says and walks back to the table.

I follow, real sick of hearing the word "fine." He doesn't talk to me for the rest of dinner or for most of prom.

▲

As Valerie said, Ethan and I take pictures, but we fail miserably at seriousness. Ethan keeps making faces, and we both crack up as we follow directions for the stupid pose the photographer makes us do.

Within twenty minutes of entering the banquet hall, three separate girls, two of whom have never spoken to me, catch me alone and ask me a question about Ethan. I answer, not thinking much of it, until the third one asks, "Tina, is he your military boyfriend?"

"No, he's just a friend of mine. How do you know about my boyfriend in the military?"

"Ya hear things," she says and walks away.

A fourth girl interrupts Ethan and me during a song. She attempts to pull me aside. I preemptively say to her, "Go tell everyone else that he's twenty three, not my boyfriend, not available, and if anyone else has questions, they can be addressed to him." I look at Ethan, who tries not to laugh. She turns red and walks off. We continue dancing undisturbed.

Valerie was right again. Ethan is a perfect gentleman and a great dancer. We have so much fun, laugh too loudly, and care nothing about how silly we are as we make up crazy dances. I abandon my shoes, and we dance to almost every song.

▲

My once-upon-a-time friend, Justin, who is best friends with Ryan, asks me to dance during a slow song. I agree because I'm curious about his motives. Fifteen seconds into the song, he starts talking.

"So, how have you been?"

"Busy," I reply.

"Busy? Okay. What have you been doing?"

"Working."

"Oh, so that's why no one has seen you around. Did you move? I drove by your house the other day, and it doesn't look like anyone lives there anymore."

"Yep."

"So, who's your date?"

"My lover," I say casually, which makes him halt, and I stifle a laugh.

"What? Is that true?" he says.

"No, Justin," I say, exasperated. "Funny, you haven't so much as looked at me for the last three months, and now all of a sudden, you're interested in my entire life. If you want intel about my date, I'm going to tell you like I told all the other silly girls…" I point to Ethan sitting at a table to my right. He sees me and waves. I continue, "There's my date right there. Go dance with him, and ask him the questions."

Justin opens his mouth, but nothing comes out. We both leave the dance floor. Ethan stands before I get to the table. "Everything all right?" he asks.

"No. High school boys are so stupid."

"I remember those days well. I used to be one of them."

A popular hip-hop song abruptly separates the close-dancing couples. "Come on," Ethan says and holds his hand out to me. "I love this song."

⋏

Another slow song starts, and the DJ announces that there are only four songs left. Andrew appears out of nowhere and taps Ethan's shoulder. Ethan steps back, and Andrew asks me to dance, but I tell him no. Ethan steps back up, and Andrew glares at him. Ethan looks at him, says, "The lady said no," and whisks me away.

"Seems like there's a lot of drama going on. You breaking hearts?" Ethan teases.

"Yeah, right. I refer back to my previous statement about boys," I say as he twirls me around.

When the song ends, we decide to leave before the last dance and split up to search for my shoes. I run into Andrew, who tries to talk to me, but I ignore him as I look under tables and chairs.

"What are you doing?" he asks.

I stop and reply, "I'm looking for my shoes."

"You're leaving? It's not even last dance yet."

"Well, I spent most of the day hungover, and now I've danced for the last three hours. I'm exhausted."

"Tina, you were drinking last night?"

"Ya know, Andrew, this is the first time in a long time we could have had fun together, but no. Why don't you go ask Justin about my life? He knows more than you at this point."

I resume the search and leave Andrew at the table, but then I see Ethan on the other side of the dance floor. He waves and holds up my shoes. "Staying Alive" and the flickering strobe lights put images of John Travolta in my head. Ethan and I disco dance to each other and meet in the middle. He offers shoes and an arm to lean on. With my feet in order and our arms linked, we dance-walk off the floor. People watch, but I don't care.

Halfway to the exit, Andrew steps in front of us, and I say, "Andrew, I have nothing to say to you."

"Tina, please wait. Can I talk to you alone?" he says and gives Ethan an impatient face.

"Tina?" Ethan asks.

After I unlink my arm, I ask Ethan to wait for me in the hallway. Once he walks away, Andrew begins, "I'm just concerned."

"Concerned, my ass! This goes way beyond concern! What the hell is your problem? It's one thing to be mad at me for not keeping in touch or whatever. It's another thing to be a complete jerk to my friend."

He doesn't answer my question, because the DJ announces last dance. He says cheerfully, "Dance with me. We have to have at least one. Come on, best friend."

"And all of a sudden, we are best friends again. If I didn't know any better, I'd swear..." I sigh, realizing the possibility, and decide not to finish the thought out loud. "Andrew, Julie is twenty feet from us. Go dance with her. I'll see you around school. Good night." I turn and walk away.

⚛

On the way home, Ethan and I laugh as we discuss the events of the evening, especially the people wanting info on him. He tells me, "Tina, I had more fun tonight than at my own prom.

In fact, it's been a while since I've had this much fun. Valerie's going to die when I tell her everything. I'm surprised she didn't try sneaking in. And don't worry about high school boys. You're right. They're all stupid anyway. Someday, you're going to make a man very happy."

CHAPTER 40

HOME

During a huge shouting match, Evelyn's marriage implodes. She immediately files for divorce and prepares to move to England. I must find somewhere else to live for the last three weeks of school.

I call the one person I should have called in the first place about a decade ago. Thanks to Mother, I haven't spoken to him in two years, and I'm nervous about his answer. Byron, my godfather—or *Ninong,* in the Tagalog language—picks me up at the end of the week.

I sit on the ground and explain things to Sasha as I run a brush through her hair. "You're going to a real home with people that can take good care of you. I'm going to Chicago for the summer, and then I'll be away at college." I hug her neck. "I'm sorry. I tried," I say and wipe away a tear. My hatred for Mother boils, but Sasha ends the thought with a paw on my arm. I shake it with a smile and tell her that a little girl will love her very much.

I am a loved little kid again. I practically spent the first seven years of my life with Byron and Vera, and I chuckle to myself, glad that some people never change. We settle into our old routine we had prior to my parents' divorce, and I wonder how different my life would have been if I had truly been their daughter.

Like military clockwork, Byron wakes me up every morning and makes my favorite breakfasts. Even though his job is in the opposite direction, he drives me to school on the other side of the river. Without fail, I exit the school building and easily find his white Ford Bronco in the same parking spot. On the way home, we discuss school and boys and college.

One afternoon, I tell him about Jonathan. He remains quiet and focused on the road ahead of us. I wonder what he's thinking and look at him as I wait for him to speak. With the exception of a few more wrinkles, he hasn't changed. Forever the perpetual tan of a redneck farmer and the smell of sunshine with a hint of motor oil and engine parts. Still handsome like Harrison Ford, with the white hair and funny bone of Johnny Carson.

Finally, he looks over at me and gives me some fatherly advice. "Tina, once you figure out life and who you are and what you want, then the right one will come along and sweep you off your feet. He may be the one you least expect, or he might be right in front of you the whole time, but you'll know because he'll make you a better person."

I think about his words and say, "I guess that makes sense," to which he replies, "It will. You'll see."

"And, Ninong, you'll be the one walking me down the aisle when the time comes."

"I don't know how your father is going to feel about that," he says with a glance.

"You've done most of the work. He'll get over it."

⁂

Vera is an excellent cook, especially with desserts and Filipino food, which I devour. During most evenings when she makes dinner, we often chat about her memories of little me and her life growing up in the Philippines. She explains Filipino culture and helps me pronounce Tagalog words.

The three of us catch up on the day's events as we eat at the kitchen table. I try not to lose my food or choke from laughing at Byron's jokes, and apparently, I'm now old enough to hear the dirty ones. I've missed the joyful spark in his bright blue eyes.

Sometimes after dinner, the three of us go for walks around the neighborhood, and he still points out the moon to me. As usual, I stand outside with him in the front yard while he finishes his cigarette. We look at the stars, or he laughs as I run around catching and releasing fireflies.

When Vera goes out for social events, Byron and I are responsible for our own dinner. Talk about the blind leading the blind. We are proud of ourselves until we get adventurous. Thirty minutes after two bites of fried chicken and seasoned rice, the pizza delivery guy rings the doorbell. We affectionately refer to that disaster as "done-done chicken and spicy rice night." From then on, we cook frozen pizza in the oven or make sandwiches. Our easy meals aren't complete unless we each have a tall glass of iced chocolate milk. On those nights, we often watch boxing, and he explains the intricacies of the sport while fluctuating between cheers and attempts to not curse.

Vera and I often go shopping, one of her favorite hobbies. I help her pick out clothes and shoes. She teaches me how to play songs on the piano, and we stay up on Friday nights watching recorded soap operas. I still wake her up when she falls asleep, and we rewind the VHS tape back to where she dozed off.

On Saturday mornings, Byron and I go for donuts at Shipley's or to breakfast at a local hole-in-the-wall with his best friend. Sometimes we go to church with Vera. On Sundays, we are up at the butt crack of dawn, he loads up the pontoon boat, and we go fishing until the heat chases us home.

During the week, I relive many of my childhood afternoons. A light drizzle begins as we take our usual places outside on the front porch. I study for my finals on the doorstep. He smokes Marlboro Reds, drinks black coffee, and reads the newspaper in the green rocking chair that has been there forever.

"Tina, why don't you get a chair? Aren't you too old to be sitting in the doorway?"

"Nope," I say, feeling absolutely content. He smiles and shakes his head.

The sky opens up. After a few minutes, I stand and stick my hand under the waterfall pouring down from the roof.

"You used to do that when you were little," he says.

"I remember, and I still do every chance I get," I say and give him a grin.

"I love you, kid."

"I love you, too, Ninong. Always and forever."

"No matter what," he replies with a wink.

CHAPTER 41

GRADUATION

The last week of school arrives, and everyone exchanges yearbooks and says goodbye to each other like we've all been best friends for the past four years. To my surprise, Justin comes up to me, gives me a hug, apologizes for his behavior, and tells me Ryan can get over himself. I accept his apology. Andrew and I finally make peace. I give him a rundown of most of the crazy shit that happened over the last four months and tell him my plan to visit Chicago.

On our final day, Andrew finds me in the hallway after the dismissal bell. As we talk on the way to the parking lot, people stop us to say goodbye and hug me or shake hands with Andrew.

"Will I see you at the senior get together?" he asks me.

"No. My family is having dinner tonight."

"Ditch them, Tina. Tonight's a night for seniors. You're going to miss out on the scavenger hunt competition."

"I would if it wasn't my entire family. My grandmother drove from Dallas with Jenny and my mom. My dad, Eric, and grandparents drove down from Chicago and arrived today."

"Oh, never mind then," he says, with understanding and a hint of disappointment.

"Is it true they're making you come back to make up the days you missed?" I ask him.

"Yeah, I have to help clean up the library or file or some other bullshit. I didn't have my best friend banging on my window so I'd get my lazy ass out of bed."

"I should have bought you a more annoying alarm clock for Christmas," I say, laughing.

"I'll see you at graduation," he says and gives me a hug.

"Yes, see you then. Have fun!"

⁂

Dressed in a red cap and gown, I wait in a two-hundred-ten-person line that snakes throughout the football stadium locker room. Andrew isn't in his spot near the front, not that I'm surprised. I keep checking the door behind me and wonder if he's the only one we are waiting for.

I'm nervous about the hundred concrete steps down to the field. Andrew and I always watched during home games for a tumbling cascade of players to begin as our team ran down to the field.

When Andrew finally passes me to take his place, he stops for a split second and whispers to me, "Don't go falling down the stairs, or I won't graduate 'cause I'll laugh myself to death." Everyone looks at me as I bellow with laughter.

We make our way to the middle of the grassy field and the rows of chairs that face the bleachers and temporary stage. Ten minutes later, my classmates and I rightfully grumble. Even though the sun is low on the horizon behind us, it's about ninety degrees, and we're all wearing at least two layers. Everyone is sweaty and out of breath. My friend Abbey makes me giggle when she whispers, "Whoever's idea this was needs to be run over by a bus."

We look at our programs and don't recognize any of the speakers except for Helen, our class president and valedictorian. Several people give nice speeches, but we become restless. Then an elderly man in uniform from the Shiner's Club makes his way slowly to the podium. I expect a resounding speech from him until he introduces himself. An "oh no" and a "goddammit" come from my fellow classmates. I search for Andrew several rows ahead of me. He turns completely around to look at me, and I bite the insides of my cheeks to contain the laughter. The little old codger is the same one we heard during an assembly earlier in the year.

I'm sure the man's speech is beautiful, but as expected, no one can understand him. If we are lucky, we hear the first two or three words of each sentence before his voice mysteriously disappears. I try to keep my face from contorting when I glance at Andrew, who turns his head around to look at me every five minutes during the entire fifteen-minute speech. When the poor guy finishes, the applause is outrageous. He says, "Oh, they really liked it," before he hobbles back to his seat.

Helen is our final speaker. Her message to the class of 1996 is short, concise, and inspiring. My eyes water from nostalgia and the possibilities of a better life.

Each row ahead of me becomes a stream of red gowns maneuvering toward the stage. When my friends' names are called, I join the chorus of cheers. Before I know it, my row is motioned to stand. Jittery with anticipation, I can't keep my body still as we inch closer and closer.

Everything becomes too surreal. I go numb when I'm next on stage. My name, and a surprising amount of cheering from the wall of bleachers, spurs me into action. Overcome with joy, I walk to the podium. I keep my eyes on the rolled parchment paper with its perfectly tied red bow and wrap my fingers around it. I fight blurry eyes as hope steps aside, and pride does the conga.

Once I leave the stage, I almost stop in my tracks. Mouth agape, I glance around. Several of my classmates stand on their feet and cheer for me. "What?" I laugh and convince my feet to keep going. I hold my head high, knowing I accomplished the impossible.

We turn our tassels and throw our caps sky-high. Everyone is a convergence of hugs, cheers, jumping up and down, and searching for caps. As quick as a flash, Ryan comes out of nowhere, hugs me, and tells me good luck in Chicago. Before I can say anything, he disappears into the crowd. I find Andrew, who picks me up with a big hug and then helps me search around.

"Well, this is it. When do you leave?" he asks as I secure my cap back onto my head.

"Tomorrow."

"Tomorrow?" he asks, and we begin our trek back to the stairs.

"Yeah, I just found out today. My dad has to get back to work. It sucks."

"Well, good luck, and have fun in Chicago."

"I will, and you have fun…back at school," I say, laughing at the last part.

"Not funny, Tina," he says, laughing with me, and then asks, "Are you going to the celebration?"

"No, my godparents are throwing me a party at their house. It will be the first time my mom and dad have been under the same roof in ten years. Should be interesting, to say the least. Speaking of, Ryan came up and hugged me just now. How did he know I was going to Chicago?"

"I may have broken our boycott and told him a few things."

"Andrew, you traitor!"

"It's graduation after all," he says with an innocent grin.

We start our assent and pause three-fourths of the way up with several other people.

"These stairs are a bastard!" I yell and stretch my ankles.

"They're not that bad," Andrew tells me.

"You're not in high heels."

"Right. They're total bastards!" he yells and stomps his foot, which makes me giggle.

We continue upward and stop momentarily inside the locker room. Once we exit, we'll be lost in the sea of families and friends.

"When are you coming back?" he asks.

"End of July the latest. I plan on being back to start in the fall."

"Knowing you, you'll probably never come back, and I do know you."

"Now you're just putting ideas in my head."

We hug one last time, and Andrew disappears.

⋏

I hesitate and stand motionless right inside the doorway. *This is it. I walk out, and my new life begins.* Red caps and gowns float past me and out into the bright lights of the stadium and the noise of the waiting crowd. With determination, I square my shoulders, shift my feet, and wiggle my toes. A big, proud smile takes over my face, and I walk through.

I'm overwhelmed. Beyond any of my expectations, my entire family greets me, including all my aunts, uncles, and cousins. Iris, Chloe, Amber, their families, and a few other friends from my old school are here as well. I've never had them all together at one time.

They engulf me with congratulations, hugs, and picture taking. My arms fill with gifts, flowers, and balloons. For a split second, in all the glorious madness, I wonder if Jonathan would have been here too.

CHAPTER 42

FREEDOM

I was the master of my own fate. To Chicago I went, and there I dwelt happily ever after.

Yeah, right.

Freedom with Father in a metropolis was its own barrel of monkeys. Meanwhile, my old life had to be dealt with. I hated Mother and my past, so what does a girl do? Therapy and medication? Nope, nope. I had an iron will and lots of practice.

Never tell. Live in denial behind barriers of shame. Never acknowledge or feel. Forget and respawn like a shiny new character in a video game. I guarded my secrets well and tiptoed around the truth with vague snippets to a few people who earned what little trust I could give.

I dug deep graves for any lingering memories, but Jonathan was the most difficult to bury. He haunted the fringes of events and conversations, as if the universe took pleasure in mocking me and recycling my old life into a different place and time with new people. I was miserable, but with practice, I learned to control my reactions until the memories became passing thoughts of a life gone by.

My little plan had an unintended consequence. Right next to Jonathan, I dug a grave for myself. Yep. I hopped right in, threw dirt on my face, and didn't even know it. I buried that girl and all her strength and wisdom.

Mother's greatest gifts remained to rule the day—two cigarette holes burned into my soul, one filled with fear and the other with self-hatred. I lived accordingly with a smiling façade until I was forced to fight for my freedom once again. I met someone who inadvertently challenged those remnants of Mother lurking inside my head. His one simple question put me on the long and winding path to healing. He said to me, "You are beautiful. You know that, right?"

CHAPTER 43

Peace

When I finally found my place in the world four years later, I successfully plowed through life, obsessively goal-oriented—college, career, husband, home, and children. All was peachy keen until life took a U-turn, and I plowed right into a road barrier.

Several losses and a rapid succession of life changes shook my core and left me raw. I felt empty, weak, and damaged. Drowning in depression, I began to examine my life to make sense of it all. Here I was, sick of being an adult at almost forty years old. How the hell did I survive my childhood?

My subconscious got hold of the memo, put on her tap shoes, and decided to Gene Kelly the inside of my skull. She had held on to that buried and ignored mountain of shit, and it was her time to shine.

All the neglected memories and feelings had festered into a malevolent force I wasn't prepared for. Horrible, painful flashes fought each other for my attention. Some quietly wandered until agitated, while most shrieked and attacked nonstop, especially at night, when I had the empty hours to obsess over every detail.

I couldn't deal, so I sought help. Meditation acted as a temporary mute button. One therapist helped me find more ghosts. Another therapist helped me understand anger, gave me helpful books to read, and encouraged me to write.

When I cracked open a spiral-bound journal of unlined, cream-colored pages, I drew a picture of myself—an image of a small and terrible seven-year-old girl whose angry face and wild eyes are hidden by her hair as she sits like a patient in a straitjacket.

From then on, I had to lock that hellion in a dark box deep within. She got too loud, clawing and screaming of betrayal and loss and pain and suffering. When I wasn't paying attention, she would escape, and I'd live in a perpetual state of flashbacks. Until I could force her back into the cage, I'd go mad with bouts of rage or depression, all directed at myself and loved ones who got in the line of fire.

Then, on an unremarkable day, I grabbed a pen and a pad of paper and began to write about someone I once loved with the intention of giving the story to my daughter at a future date. Pandora's box had opened. The little control I had over the perpetuating memories went to the wayside, and the only way I could rid myself of them was to write. And write. And write.

I relived every moment in a flood of memories and feelings that were hard to keep up with. Pen scratching across paper quickly became inadequate. My little venture into writing turned into me with a box of tissue, simultaneously typing, crying, drinking bloody marys or straight-up tequila, and listening to music well into the night. Hours turned to months. I watched as the madness and chaos in my mind arranged themselves into sentences and paragraphs across the computer screen.

With aching fingers, I tore down the walls of shame and released the pain and suffering held within. As story after story poured out, the little, angry girl in my mind grew older and was no longer a feral, cornered alley cat. The usual gibberish with snarling and gnashing of teeth became articulate, angry curses. She slowly changed into a teenager who sat quietly and patiently, interested in the stories I wrote—adding to the memories—no longer a voice of madness. She grew older still, her face becoming my face, her voice my voice, until past and present reconciled, leaving me alone in my head.

Given order and meaning, the memories lost their power and left me with a confusing emotion I couldn't identify. In the empty spaces that held all those terrible things, I found and embraced grief. Then the feeling passed, leaving me with quiet understanding and with tears on my hands, which had covered my face.

With the past stretched out on page after page, I finally grasped what my subconscious tried to tell me. I understood the magnitude and significance of my childhood, the suffering I endured, and the obstacles I overcame. I survived the circumstances I was born into through resilience and the help of the people who moved in and out of my life. Within the stories, I discovered that missing inner strength, and with it came peace.

In the calm aftermath, I dealt with the copious amounts of guilt I had for not truly protecting myself and my siblings from Mother. Why did I never tell? Why didn't I get help? Love. Loyalty. Fear. Shame. They are powerful entities.

⊥

Life slowly became a vicious circle of crazy, not crazy. We rode the merry-go-round of Mother's moods and waved at stability as we passed it by. When you grow up that way, it is hard to see, hard to know any better.

Like a witch from Oz, she switched heads at a moment's notice. She was happy, loving, and responsible. She turned selfish, hateful, and violent. Every once in a while, depression would take control, and she'd wish we weren't born, from the sanctuary of her bed. Gradually, her worst self took over; she ignored us little by little until basic parenting got tossed out a window like an abandoned shoe on a highway.

At first, my silence was out of love. I didn't question her actions and thought she knew best. When she made mistakes, she asked for forgiveness and made tear-laden promises. I gave her grace and forgave her shortcomings over and over again. Love and forgive, no matter what.

Loyalty was next in line to say "*shhhh*." I thought that if I snitched, I would betray our family and the love and trust we had for each other. I didn't want anyone to know how much trouble she was, because I didn't want her to get in trouble. I had to protect us when Mother couldn't, like it was my duty to ride out the storm and pick up the pieces until she was back to normal. Someone had to be in charge, or the family would fall apart. Take one for the team, or everyone suffered. My volunteer work led to full-time employment and mandatory overtime without pay.

Eventually, Mother used guilt and fear to keep my siblings and me in order. She told vague tales of her terrible childhood and marriage. She reminded us that she was doing her best as a single mother and that she didn't abandon us like our father. She spun a web of lies about the dangers of the outside world. The devil I knew was better than the devils my imagination created. I had to be thankful for what I had, because life could always be worse.

When we became too old for her usual runaround, she changed tactics. She bullied and ridiculed us to assert control, until her strategy escalated to full-on assaults. Fear of her and the resulting shame became intricately woven into the structure of my life. I felt ashamed to be her daughter. I felt ashamed to be me. In the dark I cowered silently, and trust became a delicate, broken little thing.

Who could I go to for help? The adults I came in contact with either didn't realize the depth of our plight or they simply minded their own business and looked the other way. If and when someone stepped up to help, Mother always won. She covered her ass with a mixture of lies and truth, or she pitched a fit, and the offending person was banished for some mundane reason. The police were useless with Mother's preemptive visits to the station or when she used her "get out of trouble for free" card, otherwise known as, my grandfather's name.

I couldn't go to my friends for help. What could they do? View and treat me differently. Pity me, or find me unworthy of friendship or love. I had convinced myself that I would be looked down on and rejected—a revolting outcast in a world of superior people.

I was isolated. No one else was like me. No one else could understand or want to understand. No one could help. My problem was too big. Mother was too powerful. I was too small and useless. I failed my family. Worst of all, I failed myself.

⋏

Once I let go of the guilt, I found that I could also forgive Mother. Ever so slowly, the good memories floated back to the surface—so few and minuscule compared to the turbulent waters of Mother out of equilibrium.

At night, she sat by my bed, played with my hair, and sang about mockingbirds and China dolls. When I was five, her mother convinced me that girls should only wear dresses. Mother sat me down and explained that girls can wear whatever they want, and we both put on a pair of blue jeans. In second grade, my teacher held to religious faith, and my class was the only one in the whole school not allowed to celebrate Easter. Mother showed up unannounced with cake, colored eggs, and baskets. She looked at my teacher and said, "What are you going to do to stop me?" and passed out treats to grabby hands. Despite the fact that she always turned red, she insisted on sunbathing smothered in tanning oil, and she did so in a bikini on a lounge chair out in the front yard.

Mother was the one who showed me how to rake fallen leaves together and jump in. Afterward, I watched her smiling face as she picked leaves out of my hair. She was the one who wrapped me in her arms, picked me up, and spun me around until we both fell over. Her hand held mine while we watched the sky and treetops spin around above us.

When the Berlin Wall toppled for all the world to see on live television, she sat on the couch next to me, with tears in her eyes. Her laughter lit up the living room as we sang and danced to the Beatles' music. She rented special movies for just the two of us, and I fell in love with the Golden Age of Hollywood.

Within all the sweet memories, I discovered a small part of me that loves the version of her that loved me properly. I realized that I repeated many of these special moments with my children.

Mother was no longer a mythical monster or storybook villain. She became a flawed human being I'll never understand. What fractured pieces of her childhood contributed to the person she became? What was it like to be a wife so young, and how did motherhood affect her? What did she go through, married to a man of a different race and religion, back when people's hearts and minds were dictated by hate?

I will never know the reasons behind her choices, actions, and behavior. I can only speculate at the cause of her madness and hope she gets help and finds peace. Above all, I am the wife and mother she could never be.

Don't get me wrong. Forgiveness wasn't the "all's forgiven, and let's be pals" kind. Oh, no. More of an "I'm letting that shit go, but I can't and won't handle your cray-cray." I remain estranged from my mother. The boundary is nonnegotiable because my concern is no longer for her feelings or well-being. She is an all-or-nothing ordeal. A relationship with her means automatic participation in her chaos. There are no exceptions, no boundaries, no loving her in compartmentalized pieces. She is an EF5 tornado—beautiful and powerful in all her glory. Best stay out of her path and love from afar. My storm-chasing days officially ended the moment I had a family, and I will continue to stay completely out of tornado alley.

⊥

I wasn't brave enough to tell as a child, because I didn't understand how much control and power I had over my own fate. Reporting neglect and abuse is easier now than it once was. Society is more aware, and people are wise enough to listen and understand. Teachers and other professionals are mandatory reporters. The internet, cell phones, and social media make a world of difference. My siblings and I imagine the evidence we could have collected and the live videos of Mother smacking us around.

All the years of feeling shame and fear kept me silent as an adult. Through writing, I accepted my past, owned it, and became better for it. I found true freedom and peace from the shame of my parents' mistakes. When my siblings are ready to share their own tales, I hope they are able to do the same.

But no matter how many times I've imagined using a telephone booth time machine, I can't go back and change my past, nor am I sure I'd want to. Thankfully, my life has turned out pretty damn well. If it was possible, I do know the one message I'd give to that little seven-year-old girl with the missing front teeth and long, wild hair:

Abuse is never yours to carry alone.

Tell someone before it breaks you.

Tell anyone and everyone before it is too late.

Tell no matter the cost.
Lights must be shined on darkness to make things right.
It won't be easy. It will be worse before it gets better.
All along I had the power to save us, and so do you.

ACKNOWLEDGEMENTS

With overwhelming gratitude, I thank my husband, Brion, who believed in me the most and gave me the time and space to create and heal. Thank you for ignoring the messy house, bringing home dinner, and keeping the kids occupied. Thank you for patience and understanding, especially when I was sleep deprived and a Princess Crabby Pants. Thank you for wiping away my tears and making me laugh when I became a hot mess of fear and doubt. Since our beginning, eighteen years ago, you have always helped me become a better person.

To my children, Ray and Evan, who taught me what it means to be a mommy and helped heal my greatest wounds- you are my masterpieces. I love you always and forever, no matter what!

Thank you, Ma and Dad Fitz, for being wonderful grandparents and for the endless hours of babysitting so that I could work on this book and keep my sanity.

Eric and Jenny supported me every step of the way! Thank you for leaving your comfort zones and helping me delve into the past. I'm so grateful for our bond and daily conversations. Your words of wisdom and laughter carried me throughout. Jen, you are a talented photographer! Thank you for helping me with all things social media.

My godparents taught me the true meaning of family. They gave me the foundation of unconditional love upon which I was able to stand and become the person I am today. Byron and Vera, I modeled my life from your examples, and I hope I have made you proud.

Jonathan, I am eternally grateful for your love all those years ago. You are my knight in shining armor, and you will always have a special place in my heart.

Aunt Jackie, wherever you may be, know that I will forever appreciate your kindness and guidance during those terrible years. Thank you for helping me survive. I miss you.

Iris, Chloe, Amber, and Andrew are the special chosen few who gave me some of my best childhood memories. Even though we have grown apart, I'll never forget you or what our friendship meant.

Thank you to book club members Kristine Benavides, Michelle Young, Loyda Overton, Jaysen Fitzgerald, and Zahadul Hoque. Your feedback, critiques, and suggestions were instrumental in helping me improve my manuscript. Michelle, thank you for being my first reader and for encouraging me to share my story with the world. Kristine, you have been my best friend for almost my entire adult life. Thank you for being my number one fan. I couldn't have wished for a better-chosen sister.

A special thank-you to my editor, Mindi; publishing consultant, Jennifer; and the talented team of designers at Elite Authors whose expertise and careful attention transformed my manuscript into a polished work of art.

Of course, none of this would be possible without the generosity of my Kickstarter tribe especially Kristine and Arvin Benavides, Sean and Loyda Overton, Crystal and Joey Colton, Micheal Carmouche, Marie and Ogden Fitzgerald, Joe and Anna Stornello, Eric and Shirley Razote, Peter Sullivan, Jennifer and Bobby Dixon, Joe and Jamie West, Atul and Hema Jha, Jaysen Fitzgerald, and Brion Fitzgerald. Thank you for believing in me and cheering me past the finish line.

Made in the USA
Middletown, DE
22 February 2021